BURR
JOURN
·WEST·

George Cunningham

Photographs
Brian Redmond
Design
John Dixon

First Published 1980 by
Shannonside Mid-Western Regional Tourism Organisation
The Granary, Michael Street,
Limerick

Printed in the
Republic of Ireland by
Limerick Leader (Printing) Ltd.,
54 O'Connell Street, Limerick.
Typesetting by
Typeset Ltd., Dublin.
© George Cunningham 1980
ISBN 0 9503080 2 1

Introduction

Burren Journey West, as the title implies, travels through the coastal region of the Burren in north west Clare, and is in the nature of a sequel to the 1978 publication, *Burren Journey,* which explored the heart of the Burren.

Again, directions are given from one place to the next, rather than from a central point, so that the journey can start at any site, with no loss of continuity. Kilfenora, because of the Display Centre, is once more the starting point, this time of a figure-of-eight route with Lisdoonvarna situated in the middle. There are detours suggested to many places of interest near the main road. A visit to some of these is strongly recommended, not least because a walk across the limestone pavements and the terraced hills adds to your understanding of this unique landscape.

Burren Journey West follows a lengthy route. For some it will be a quick glance from the roadside at the accessible antiquities; for others the journey may form the basis of a holiday. The route may be divided into nine main sections, each of which could be comfortably explored in a day.

1. Kilfenora and Lisdoonvarna
2. Ballinalackan, Oughtdarra and Ballynahown
3. Fanore and the Caher Valley
4. Black Head and Gleninagh
5. Ballyvaughan, Aillwee Cave and Corkscrew Hill
6. Slieve Elva, Killeany and Kilmoon
7. Kilshanny, Ennistymon, Lahinch and Liscannor
8. Corney's Country and the Cliffs
9. Doonagore, Doolin and Knockfin

Whatever way you decide to travel through the Burren I hope that the experience will be refreshing. As you explore, please treat these works of God and Man with respect and so ensure their survival for future generations.

ACKNOWLEDGEMENTS

All archaeological drawings are based on the work of T. J. Westropp. The Lawrence photographs are reproduced courtesy of the National Library of Ireland and the Clare County Library. The encouragement and assistance of Shannonside staff, particularly Sean Browne and Brendan Russell is gratefully acknowledged, as is the help received from the Burren Centre, Michael Vaughan and all my many friends in North West Clare.

Sincere thanks to Brian Redmond for his marvellous photographs and to Gay Treacy, his pilot for the aerials, and also to John Dixon, the designer, for all his expertise.

I am particularly grateful to Very Rev. Laurence Walsh O. Cist., John Feehan, Tom McCarthy and Lucia McCarthy who commented on the typescript and helped with the proofs. Finally I owe immense gratitude to Carmel who helped at all stages, and to Paul and Brian who had to climb over rocks when, maybe, they should have been building sandcastles. Safe journey.

G. C., May 1980

Kilfenora

Kilfenora is situated at the southern tip of the Burren. Although the population is barely over a hundred, the small village continues to be a focal point for Burren development. Local initiative, backed by state-sponsored bodies, dispelled the apathy, and remedied some of the neglect of the fifties and sixties. But too many derelict and uninhabited buildings still detract from the village landscape, for, potentially at least, Kilfenora is a charming place. Few villages in Ireland have its visitor attractions and wide public spaces.

Our journey starts at Kilfenora in a walkabout fashion commencing with the Display Centre in the Market Square. Then a short circular walk through the cathedral and churchyard, past the crosses, will bring you to the Catholic church. Here, you may decide to take the short detours offered, before returning up the village street to the square.

Burren Display Centre

Most Irish people have at least heard of Kilfenora. To many, its famous ceili band was a household name. To others, Kilfenora meant the cathedral and High Crosses. Now, because of the Display Centre, the village is very well-known as a visitor interpretative gate-way to the Burren. Certainly, if this is your first visit to the region, the Centre will help to give a basic understanding of the Burren and its prominent features.

Housed within the small building are the interpretative centre, craft shop, reference library and tea-rooms. The centrepiece is a scale model of a composite Burren landscape which, with effective lighting and commentary, explains the geology and settlement patterns of the area. Prominently displayed around the walls are silk and wax recreations of the flora and fauna. Also on display are local artifacts, and replicas of other artifacts housed elsewhere.

Looking west over Kilfenora

The centre, which was officially opened by President O'Dalaigh in 1975, is managed by Comhar Conradh na Boirne, and continues to be developed by them. This co-operative is also attempting ancillary schemes to improve the quality of life in the neighbourhood.

A visit to the centre is a must.

Kilfenora Cathedral

Kilfenora is the episcopal capital of the Diocese of Kilfenora, which is one of the smallest diocese in Ireland, having only thirteen parishes. St. Fachtnan is the patron saint, but little is known of the monastery prior to the 12th century, when it seems to have been stung to almost feverish activity following the Synod of Rathbreasail in 1111, where Kilfenora's claim to separate episcopal government was ignored. As the diocese is almost coterminous with the two baronies of Burren and Corcomroe, the tribal lands

15th century window in the south wall of the chancel.

The mitred head and shoulders of a bishop

of O'Loghlen and O'Connor, it may well have been these chieftains who insisted on the retention of their bishopric, to the exclusion of the O'Brien-favoured See of Killaloe. We can only conjecture that the building of the cathedral and carving of the crosses took place at that time, more or less staking a claim to episcopal independence. These efforts paid off, for the Synod of Kells in 1152, under Cardinal Paparo, recognised Kilfenora – Fenaborensis in Latin – as a suffragan of Cashel. Following the disendowment of the monasteries in the 16th century, the small size and scattered population of the diocese caused constant financial problems, allowing Lord Stafford to say in 1638 that .... "The old Bishop of Kilfenora is dead and his bishopric, one of those which when it falls goes begging for a new husband, being not worth above four score pounds to the last man."

Today the See is joined to Killaloe in the Church of Ireland episcopacy, and in the Roman Catholic union, Bishop Casey of Galway is the Apostolic administrator. Pope John Paul II is the present Bishop of Kilfenora.

The cathedral was of a nave and chancel type, but in the last century the nave became the present Church of Ireland, detached completely from the chancel, so allowing this latter part to be conserved as a National Monument. As you walk from the stile you face the south wall, and east is to the right. Proper orientation now will help in locating the various points of interest.

The Chancel

A 15th century door leads into the chancel where we walk to the left to take a general look around: east window, tomb niche, effigies, cross shaft and tomb-slabs – all will repay close attention to their detail. Dominating the scene is the transitional three-light east window with its triangular pillars topped by carved capitals of dwarf clerics and foliage, and framed by a rounded arch with mouldings ending in serpents. These now look like eagles.

On your left the tomb niche is sometimes referred to as a sedilia, but the openings between the pilasters are too narrow for well-fed medieval clerics. These pillars support a high pointed arch filled with attractive cusped tracery. The head of a bishop, mitred, one point in front and two behind, was inserted over this. Lately placed in its present position beside the niche, is an incised tomb slab showing a

One of the carved capitals of the east window.

The cusped tracery of the wall-tomb with the bishop's head.

bishop vested for mass, mitred with ornmental browband, and holding an out-turned crozier of Irish form.

Two effigies are placed on either side of the east window. To the north is the effigy of a bishop, carved in low relief, on a rectangular slab within a cusped niche; he is vested, and has a ring on the right hand raised in blessing. The other effigy is that of a cleric, tonsured and bare-headed, dressed for choir and holding a book. These sculptures can all be dated to the 14th/15th century and have affinity with carvings of co-eval date in the Franciscan Friary, Ennis. Notice the broken cross shaft set in the chancel floor. Worth noting too, are the medieval tombs, one being that of Neptune Blood, whose only claim to fame now is that he was the uncle of Colonel Blood, whose attempt to steal the crown jewels secured for him a place in history.

The door in the north wall leads into the sacristy or chapter room, which was originally of two storeys. It seems to be of the same date as the main building, although no binding occurs. Three windows on the east side, two of the lancet type and one ruinous two-light, remain. Walk out into the graveyard, notice the huge boulders used in the north wall as you come around to the west front. The buttress you pass seems to add to the awkwardness of the front, which has been harshly described as, 'a pile of emigrants' luggage with a rabbit hutch or bird cage overhead.'

The High Crosses

Kilfenora is seldom spoken of without mention of its crosses. Tradition speaks of seven, while modern references list between three and seven, all 12th century and all of limestone. Facing the west front is the Doorty cross, one of the puzzling pieces of Irish Romanesque.

The unfinished cross in the north-west corner of the graveyard.

A simple cross stands in the northwest corner of the graveyard; it looks almost like a trial piece. Near the Catholic church the most imposing example is seen. One cross was removed to Killaloe by Dr. Mount in 1821 and can be seen in the cathedral there. These crosses are complete but there are fragments too: a cross shaft in the chancel, and another outside the present door of the church; and cross fragments at the south wall of the chancel, and perhaps another beside the west wall of the sacristy.

The Doorty Cross

This most enigmatic of crosses lay for centuries in two separate pieces, until the 1950s, when Liam de Paor realised the connection and had the cross raised. The east side shows Christ with conical mitre as Abbot of the world, directing his abbots on earth to destroy the bird – depicting

The shaft of the Doorty Cross showing the unusual figures on the south side.

the devil – who is busily attacking and devouring some unfortunate soul. Notice how Christ is extending two fingers downwards in blessing and is holding a Continental-type crozier (lack of Irish confidence?).
The other two abbots are holding a Tau crozier and one of Irish type.

On the west face a fully clothed crucified Christ is surrounded by birds. The lower panels are covered with intricate, coarse animal interlace, its end thread held over the shoulder by a man on horseback, as he gallops over a tiled surface. Alternatively, it may be depicting Christ's triumphant entry into Jerusalem. Strange figure carving is noticed on the south side of the cross.

The graveyard also has some interesting tomb slabs. See if you can find the tombstone of Patrick Lysaght (died 1741 at the age of 85) with the epitaph:

"Marti et Baccho saepe tributa dedi".

Mars and Bacchus are given a local interpretation in the following translation: 'I paid my respects to faction fights and poteen'.

The tallest of the crosses is in a field near the Catholic church.

The Nave

Normally the church is locked, but the key is obtainable locally. Over the door protrudes the mitred head and shoulders of a bishop; beside it stands the shaft of a narrow cross with interlacing. Inside, steps lead up from the porch and vestry to the belfry. Considerable alterations took place when the nave became the detached church: side aisles were levelled, the chancel arch became the new east window and other windows were opened. Little of antiquarian interest now remains in the nave, save for a corbelled head, a font and a late 17th century tomb. The head is the work of an expert carver, but the McDonagh tomb, with obelisks and armorial bearings, is, according to Westropp, in the poorest classical taste. A second McDonagh tomb was removed, but the present monument survived when the family challenged the Established Church in the High Court and won.

In a field circa 100 metres from the graveyard gate, stands the tallest of the crosses. It is four metres high on a limestone plinth, showing on the east side a fully clothed crucified Christ standing on two ropes which are joined as a V. These continue down the shaft and then divide into a larger V. Interlacing and other motifs decorate the other side.

By The Catholic Church

St. Fachtna's Catholic church (1917) is built in simple T plan with round-headed door, rose window and bellcote. To the right at the church the minor road leads to Kilshanny and on to Doolin. On this road, in a field to the left, at the edge of the village, can be seen Cashlaunavogga,

Caislean a' Mhagaidh, the fake, unfinished castle about which nothing is known. The main entrance to Ballykeel House is three tenths of a mile (0.5 km) further to the right. Then comes Fanta Glebe House, and two and a half miles (4 kms) from the village, Smithstown Castle which is well sited on the left.

Smithstown Castle

Smithstown (or Ballingown) was an O'Brien stronghold. It had an attached house inhabited up to 1837 but now destroyed. In 1600 Hugh O'Donnell rested here before pushing on through Kilfenora to lay waste the countryside around Corcomroe. Honora, daughter of Teige, the owner of Smithstown, became Honora Wingfield, ancestor to the Lords Powerscourt. The towerhouse retains interesting features in its windows, stairs and carved chimney-piece.

Back at Kilfenora the road left by the church goes to Ennistymon. At the edge of the village beyond Kilcarragh House – behind Kilfenora school – are the foundations of an ancient hospital. We return to the Burren centre through the village. Beside the craft shop the road leads to Lickeen lake, where there is good coarse fishing.

The road to Lisdoonvarna

Check your mileage in the square. From Kilfenora the road to Lisdoonvarna goes through the shale uplands, of mainly heavy soil, with bog and some newly planted forest. At the village edge is the old fair green with its castellated pay stand. The road to Ballyvaughan via Caherballykinvarga, Noughaval and Corkscrew Hill is the route of the first Burren Journey.

Ballyshanny ruined castle, built within a caher or ring-fort, is four tenths of a mile (0.6 km) from the village; now visible from the road are its grass-topped vaulted lower storey and traces of two upper floors. Originally an O'Brien castle, the proprietor in 1641 was Daniel O'Shanny, Dean of Kilfenora.

Two tenths of a mile (0.3 km) from Ballyshanny, the outhouses seen on the left, formed part of Ballykeel estate, one of the few 'big houses' in north west Clare. George Lysaght of Woodmount, Ennistymon built a house here in the late 18th century. This was followed in the early 19th century by a more classical house of cut stone with a central bow, the home of the Blake Fosters. A modern bungalow, almost on the door-step of the big house, became the residence in our times.

We travel through the bog and Ballygastell wood. The shortest way to the strand at Fanore is to take the track to the right, three and a half miles (5.6 km) from Kilfenora. After one kilometre of gravel you meet the tarred road at the site of Judge Comyn's house. Heading north by Slieve Elva this will eventually bring you through the Caher valley to the sea.

Coming into Lisdoonvarna

The houses in the small estate at the outskirts of Lisdoonvarna were built in 1975 by a voluntary group, RHO. The Rural Housing Organisation was set up in 1972 to bring new life to rural villages, by providing houses for young families at reasonable cost. On average the houses this group provide are some 30% cheaper than the commercial equivalent. To date nearly 500 houses have been completed in thirty five villages, mainly west of the Shannon, by this voluntary but highly skilled group.

Almost next door, on the site of the old Atlantic Hotel, the Stella Maris Convent and convalescent home was opened in 1954 by a French congregation, the Sisters of Our Lady of Evron. To-day the sisters continue the good work, caring full time for almost fifty elderly people.

As we approach the T junction the townland name, Knockaunvicteera, the little hill of the wolves, reminds us of long-gone problems.

Lisdoonvarna and its Wells

Straight on is the bog road to Ennistymon; we are turning right up Sulphur Hill and then left at the square for Black Head.

Lisdoonvarna is a small village with a population of just over 750. It grew from early in the 19th century around its spa wells, to become famous as a health resort, and now is the only operating spa in these islands. There were four wells:

a) Copperas Well, on the Kilmoon stream behind the Post Office is now closed. The Waters were used externally for skin diseases, ulcers and sores. It enjoyed a wide local reputation.
b) The Magnesia and Iron Well beside the stream is opened during the season.
c) The Twin Wells of iron and sulphur to the rear of the pitch and putt course.
d) The main Sulphur Well here at the bottom of the hill in a very picturesque setting.

All the waters contain iodine, with the sulphur spring being richest and free from any undue proportion of purgative salts; mineral salts make the water palatable.

Growth of the Spa

Contrary to popular opinion Lisdoonvarna was much visited before 1845, the official birth of the spa. Hely Dutton in his 1808 Clare Survey could say:

'Lisdoonvarna has been long celebrated for its virtues, particularly in obstructions,

At the Twin Wells

and some find it beneficial after a winter's drinking of bad whiskey from private stills; strongly ferruginous, and of an astringent taste and strong smell,but not fetid. The spa would be much resorted, if accommodation for drinkers could be had, but the health of those who go there is probably more injured by damp, dirty lodgings in cabbins, than benefited by the use of the water. Evidently leases of sufficient length for building could not be obtained, and this accounted for the lack of decent accommodation.

Another early visitor tells: 'on gout the sulphur has a decidedly good effect, much being dependent on the habits of the individual .... (these sufferers) defeat the object by indulging in viands so poisonous to a gouty system as lobster, salmon and champagne.'

Lewis in 1838 could inform us that the water had long been celebrated for its efficacy in visceral complaints. Hely Dutton would have been pleased with the traveller's report of 1888: 'The hotels vie with each other in contributing to the comforts of their patrons and the United Kingdom does not possess a health-resort so well favoured in this regard. The charges at the various hotels range from eight shillings and sixpence to a half-guinea per head per diem (42p to 52p), and the catering is excellent and leaves nothing to be desired'.

High praise indeed, added to by an 1891 tourist: 'and while the rich and humbler class meet here, as in the world at large, the wants of all are provided for according to their rank and station, and their ability to pay for extra comforts.'

The complaint at this time concerned the taking of the waters: conditions were primitive. The wells were owned by the Guthrie family, with an almost legendary figure, Biddy the Sulphur, dispensing the libations. Again the 1888 traveller: 'The water is served out free of charge in a neat little pump-house by an attendant who rejoices in the name of 'Biddy', now quite a household word at the spas. More modern and improved methods of dispensing the water might, with advantage, be instituted and Biddy might be content to earn a well-merited repose.'

Later, a Dr. Westropp became the owner of the property. He developed the wells and added baths. His private residence on the hill overlooks the spa. The odd turrett of this house, which had an outside spiral staircase, was built to give a view of the sea.

Expansion

Lisdoonvarna continued to expand and prosper during the twentieth century, one writer in 1920 telling us that Lisdoon' 'is the Homberg of Irish priests,' and a 1952 traveller telling of 'this highly respectable town, mostly frequented by well-to-do people who 'take the waters' and look solemnly and searchingly at one another.'

Looking down on the deep gorges of the streams at Lisdoonvarna.

Farmers, especially bachelors, flocked here when the harvest was completed, both for a rest and for the very serious matter of acquiring a wife. The place became a matchmaker's paradise as countless marriages were contrived, signed and sealed, tight as any international merger. To-day there is hardly a matchmaker to be found and the young have taken over, especially at night time when they pour in for the 'crack'.

The Modern Spa

The wells continue to attract large numbers: the Spa complex is certainly different and well worth a visit. Saunas, solarium, keep-fit equipment and a well designed recreation centre have recently been added. The pump-house with all its Victorian gear and fittings still dispenses glasses of the sulphurous water for a modest consideration. I found it a never-to-be-repeated experience, but I am told that the smell grows on you. The park area at the confluence of the Gowlaun and the Aille is pleasantly landscaped with an other-world atmosphere prevailing.

Lisdoonvarna Failte Ltd., a local community-dominated company owns the complex, the park on both sides of the road, and a sizable parcel of surrounding land. Across the road (Sulphur Hill) the 30 acres – formerly the grounds of Rathbaun House – encircled by its streams, contain a football field, an 18 hole pitch and putt course, a town pavilion, and walks leading to the Twin Wells beyond the confluence of the Kilmoon and Aille streams. Here, springing from one rock, within a couple of inches of one another, are two wells, one sulphur, the other iron . . . 'side by side which, both in taste and smell, are as distinct as if miles asunder.' The once-cared-for well-house is now in a ruinous condition.

In the village, the mid-19th century Catholic church is of Victorian hard gothic with 20th century additions, particularly the modern entrance. From the town square the road east goes to St. Brendan's Well, which we will visit on our return journey. Down Canon's Hill to the west is our route to the sea and Black Head.

On your right at the bottom of the hill, behind an iron wrought fence and swinging side gate, are the Iron Wells accommodated in what was once a neat little pump-house, with an attractive fireplace. Copperas Well was farther up the stream; notice the deep gorge which the waters have cut through the shale.

At the crossroads on the outskirts of Lisdoonvarna, veer right for Black Head – first left is to Ennistymon and straight on is to Doolin – travelling through the shales, which used be called the Coal Measures.

Ballinalackan

Iron Age Burial Places

One and a half miles (2.4 kms) from the Doolin turn-off, just as the sea ahead comes into view, three Iron Age (500 B.C. - 500 A.D.) burial mounds, called ring or bell barrows are to the right of the road, one at the highest point. These and many others in this district point to a considerable settlement of the early Celts. The most westerly barrow was called the Mote – the term now given to a Norman fortified mound, a motte – but Westropp recognised it to be sepulchral in origin. Although cut through by a field fence, and with some surface digging evident, the burials are probably intact.

Nearer the road, 125 metres to the east is Lislard, the second of the barrows. It is two-tiered, and of considerable size, with a wide fosse, but this does appear to have been spoiled. Further to the east is the smallest barrow. It is really conjectural to call these earthworks Iron age burials as excavation could show both a different purpose and age. As far as I

The burial mound of Craggycorradan East.▶

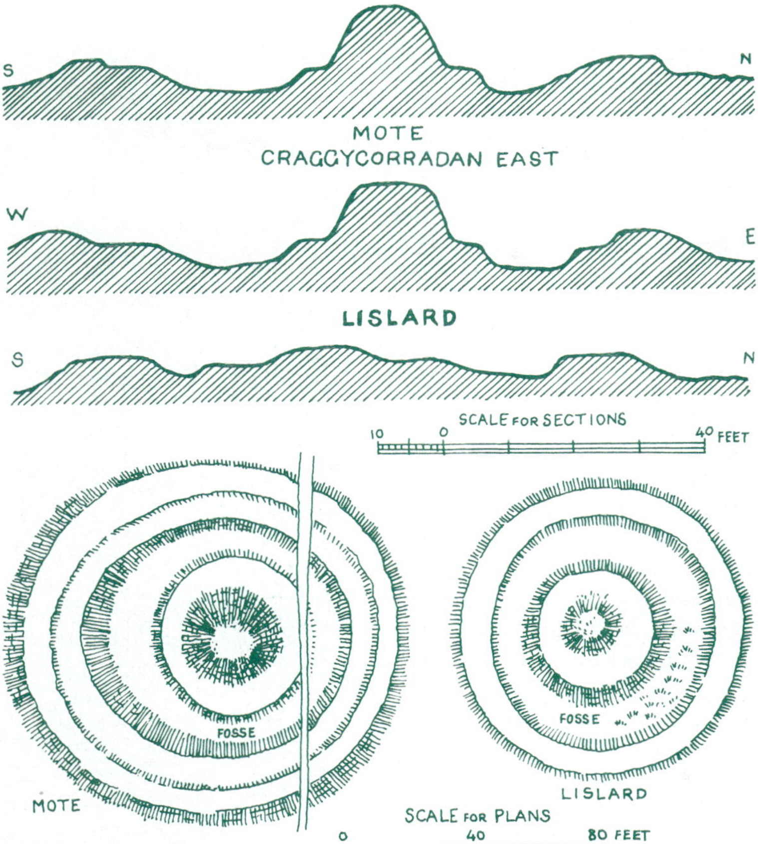

Graggycorradan and Lislard

know, the nearest similar excavated barrow was at Oran Beg, Co. Galway, and this revealed cremated burials in the silted-up fosse, accompanied by grave goods including bone beads and bronze fibulae. The central mound in the barrows is in the nature of a monument, maybe for commemoration or to foil grave robbers. Also, it is well to remember that the burial could be dedicatory, and that there is no clear dividing line between ring barrows and earth circle ritual sites.

The View

Pull off the road as the view unfolds to give, on a clear day, a memorable vista. Straight ahead the Aran Islands, with Inisheer in the foreground, seem only a stone's throw away. To your right Ballinalackan castle, looking impregnable, stands guard over the valley; and beyond, the rock gardens and terraced limestone hills of Oughtdara and Ballynahown meet the shale land of Knockauns. To all this, obedient to the elements, the east-bent woodlands form a carpeted preface. Below in the valley, to the left, Poll an Ionian, the cave with Europe's longest

Ballinalackan tower-house showing the machicolation on top guarding the entrance.▶

Ballinalackan's strategic positioning could hardly have been bettered.

stalactite, is entered at the foot of the cliff. South, beyond Doolin, the sea edge rises in ridges to culminate in the Cliffs of Moher.

All this district of Corcomroe was held from early times by the O'Connors who had a common ancestry with the O'Loghlens, chiefs of Burren. Owing to family feuding the O'Connor inheritance slipped away. By 1566 the Four Masters could tell that the territory of Corcomroe was granted to Donal O'Brien; and in 1582 Boetius Clancy witnessed the formal granting of these lands to the O'Briens. This Boetius was the chief brehon (justice) whose bardic school was down the valley at Knockfin, and whose signature was essential for the validity of any legal document in Thomond (i.e. North Munster). More about Boetius when we visit Doolin.

The formal granting of these lands on behalf of the Queen was made in 1585 to Turlough O'Brien; excluded were Boetius' lands and the property of the Bishop and Dean of Kilfenora. Tooclae, Tuath Glae, was the old name for this immediate area.

Our next stop is the castle and villa (signposted); then we make a detour into the valley and uplands beyond, before we continue north by the sea to Black Head. Doolin, Knockfin and the cliffs we will visit from the south at the end loop of our journey.

Peter the Packer's Castle

The key to Ballinalackan Castle is available at the guesthouse. After granting unlimited access for many years, continued vandalism forced the proprietor to erect and lock an iron door, but visitors are always welcome to this important and well preserved tower-house. As it was an O'Brien stronghold most of the surviving features seem to date from the middle 1500's when they obtained undisputed control over this district; however, it could have superseded an earlier fortification. Daniel O'Brien of Dough, Lahinch held it in 1641-1642, and in 1654 a Cromwellian officer ordered the dismantling masons to spare the 'strand hasse at Dough and the castle at Ballinalackan until further orders.' By the Act of Settlement in 1667 a Captain Hamilton became proprietor, but the O'Briens regained possession. In the 19th century John O'Brien, claiming descent from Turlough O'Brien, inherited or bought the property.

The bawn, an enclosed defended courtyard, is entered through a later, corbelled, machicolated gateway; notice how the cliff edge has been additionally fortified with a row of limestone boulders. I wonder did they ever need them. That cliff face over Poulnagun looks formidable. Westropp, at the turn of the century, wrote of a corbelled pier of a postern gate, which was at the north-eastern corner of the bawn.

The tower-house appears to be in two sections, albeit built at the same time, as evidenced by the masonry, and bonded later. Much narrower, and rising a storey higher than the main wing, the entrance block is to the east, with the doorway defended by a top machicolation. On the ground floor this slim tower has a porter's lodge or store room on the left facing the

Ballinalackan *Fireplace.*

circular stairs before you enter the bottom room of the main wing. Over the porter's lodge are three storeys of bedrooms, all lit by small ogee-headed windows; the top storey leads up to the wall walk and had a west window now closed by the ledge of a lower roof of later date.

Under that roof the main wing had four storeys. An intermural passage (now over a holed arch) at first floor level led to a garderobe or necessarium in the south wall. The floor over the vault has a defaced fireplace, much inferior to the finely carved Tudor chimney, inscribed 1641, in the upper room; this chimney was probably a later insertion. These vaults retain the marks of the wicker hurdles over which they were turned. At the top a doorway leads to the machicolation on the north wall and another to the now inaccessible machicolation facing west. These all rest on corbels and have round musket holes, two to the outer face and one to each side. There are extensive views from any of the upper rooms.

A machicolation fortified with musket holes.

Ballinalackan House

The mid-19th century bow fronted bungalow is thought to have been built by John O'Brien, a son of the second wife of Cornelius O'Brien M.P., about whom we will be hearing a lot later. John was the father of Lord Peter O'Brien, (1842-1914), better known as Peter the Packer from the packed juries he engineered to secure the desired verdict. The front lounge has a distinctive marble fireplace carved from a single slab and a circular, centre-roof window. Some stained glass and a stone crest of the O'Briens also survive from the original residence, which became a guest house in 1938. The castle is popularly known as that of Peter the Packer.

Oughtdarra

The first major detour of our journey, is the road, right immediately beyond the entrance to Ballinalackan castle, to the valleys of Oughtdarra and the uplands of Ballynahown. These are fascinating places where one could spend a whole holiday and still not see everything. If you are pushed for time, or do not particularly want to walk through the crags, the two mile (3.2 kms) drive to the end of the tarred road is worthwhile, if only for the view: the castle appears in a new light and the islands, 'fort-crowned and church-crowded', begin to show their individuality.

For those of us who like 'a spot to linger out a dreamy summer day' there is a little of everything to see. Drive past the first right turn; this road goes, by Ballinalackan National School (built 1840-closed 30th June 1979), back to Lisdoonvarna.

Oughtdarra

Take the first left turn for Oughtdarra and travel seven tenths of a mile (1.1 km) on this narrow road to the last bend. To the right, around the hillock in the deepest valley, is the secluded religious site of St. MacDara. It was in use up to recently as a killeen – here a burial place both for unbaptised children and for those under seven years of age. The derivation of Oughtdarra from St. MacDara is doubtful, as the following old spellings demonstrate: Waffering is what appears in the 1302 Papal Taxation; Owghtory, given as a separate parish to Killilagh in 1584, and Ughdara in a 1655 map.

The very ruined church measured some

6m x 12m and was sited in a seven acre walled enclosure, part of which is now locally called the Orchard. As bones were constantly turning up, the owners of the land, the Kellehers, ceased tilling the immediate area. One 16th century coin also surfaced, but finds from the Burren – 'flint weapons, bronze ornaments, moulds for a bronze spear, iron coins of the Plantagenets and Tudors' – all are most equivocal and tell no chronological story.

Fauna

A common sight on the land at Oughtdarra are the nanny goats. Their presence does make sense and we may see a return to greater numbers on Irish farms, for some farmers have found it a bonus to run a couple with their dairy herd, as they are the best of weedkillers. Besides the goats can suckle calves extremely well. These nannies are no relation to the feral goats, the biggest wild animals in these parts. You may see them roaming the uplands eating the winterage so carefully nurtured and prized by the local farmers.

In these sheltered valleys and particularly in Ballyryan, the adjoining valley to the west, are found the shyer forms of Irish mammals: badgers, foxes, stoats and pine martens. All have a fairly safe habitat in this area, noted internationally by zoologists. As the Burren arboreal is one of its strongholds, the pine marten (Martes martes) deserves special mention. This rarely-seen animal is similar to but larger than a stoat or ferret, almost like a cat with a bushy tail, feeding on birds, birds' eggs and smaller animals. Its distinctive features are a chocolate-coloured coat, white throat and chest patch. As its coat of fur is much valued, humans are the pine martens' greatest enemy. Abroad it is also called the sweet marten to distinguish it from its cousin, the polecat or foul marten.

The Burren is also a meeting place for lepidopterists (experts on butterflies and moths) as here twenty six of Ireland's thirty three species have been recorded; also, one moth discovered here in 1949, and named Burren Green, is not found elsewhere in these islands. And if your fancy runs to snails, we have some rare ones for you!

On the limestone pavements at Ballynahown, with the Cliffs of Moher in the distance.

Fact and Legend

Westwards from Oughtdarra is the fairy hill of Croghateeaun (Cruach An tSidheain), crowned by a small but strong fort. North from this, on the cliff edge, is the inland promontory fort of Doonaunmore: a strong wall, three metres in height and thickness, and one hundred metres long, fortifying the neck of the headland, with the remains of houses inside. Legends tell that the giant who lived there was overthrown when he lost his magic staff, and that a cairn in the townland, called the giant's grave, was destroyed in the belief that he lay with his sword beside him.

The Green Road

Return to the T junction, turn left and continue for one and three tenth miles (2.1 kms) to the last house on your right. Drive on, if you like, to the end of the gravelled road, but you will have difficulty turning. Soon we will walk seawards to visit some wedge tombs and the stone fort at Caherdoon.

Before you meet the Green Road, notice, on your left, the disused lime kiln, a very common sight in the shale districts, particularly near a bog. Many of these were in use up to recent times, manuring and improving the poor, sour land. Nearly all of these are running kilns, built into a hillside so that the broken stone and fuel could be tipped in with the least trouble; a stone-built bowl tapered downwards to the bottom, from where the lime and ashes were drawn. This is a very poor example.

You may like to walk for a while along the Green Road, one of the old Burren highways. From here it skirts the western slopes of Slieve Elva, passes by Faunarooska Castle, crosses over the mountain to dip into the Caher Valley at Formoyle; then up the northern slope past Caheranardurrish, down into Feenagh valley by Rathborney, and around the mountain by Corcomroe Abbey to Corker Pass.

At various stages of the track are traces of settlement which may be late medieval. About one mile (1.6 km.) from here is the curious group of ring walls of various

Details of forts near Ballinalackan, Co. Clare.

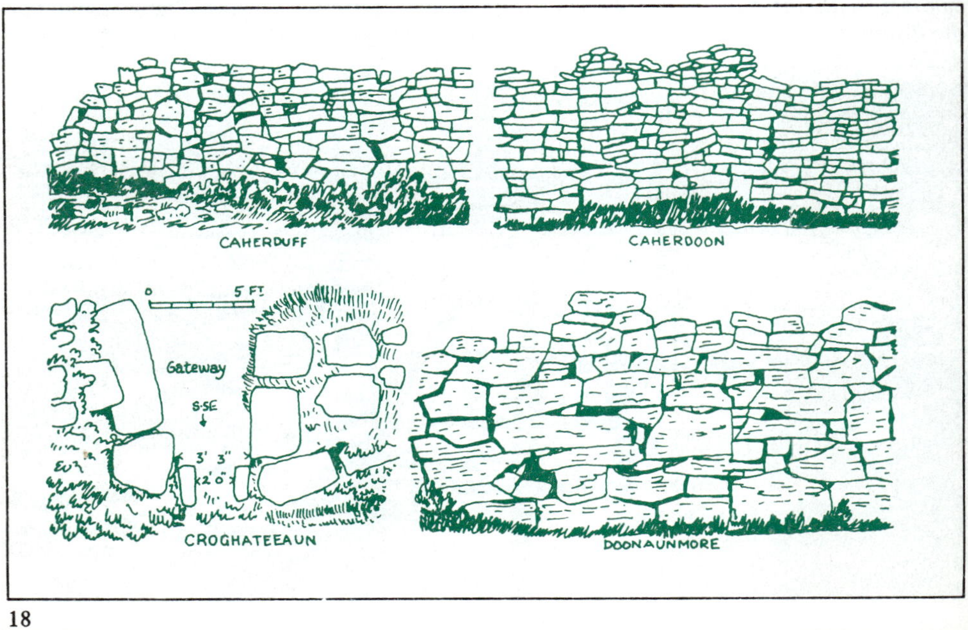

size and age at Liscoonera, Cahermoyle and Caherbeg. They may be late bawns, degenerate descendents of the real cahers. One half mile (.8km) on the right is the entrance pot-hole to Poulnagree, at 1.2km, the longest cave on the west side of Knockaunsmountain.

Ballynahown

It is now proposed to visit the wedge tombs of Ballynahown and the nearby stone fort. The tombs, except for one, are ruinous. If you just want to see some wedge tombs, there are others, more easy of access, elsewhere in the Burren. However the walk, although a little hazardous, owing to the uneven terrain, is worth the effort for the flora, the bracing air and the splendid scenery.

Near where the Green Road commences, follow the boundary wall seawards for about ½ Km. Then, south of the wall, you will meet the uninteresting remains of Ballynahown North wedge tomb in a two metre deep natural hollow, with the west wall, four metres long surviving. Keep going west a further ½ Km. to the stone fort.

Flora

I hope you are walking across these limestone pavements in late Spring or early Summer when the plants, Arctic, Alpine and Mediterranean are at their best. Then the Spring Gentian *(Gentiana verna)*, Mountain Avens *(Dryas octapetala)* and some orchids turn these fields into blazing rock gardens. You might be lucky enough to discover the delicate Maidenhair Fern *(Adiantum–capillus veneris)* from the Mediterranean, with its shining black leaf-stalks and pale green leaflets.

In late Summer the purple-red Bloody Cranesbill – the jewel of the Burren – dominates the rock, and everywhere there are orchids. This botanists' paradise can survive only if its greatest threat, careless

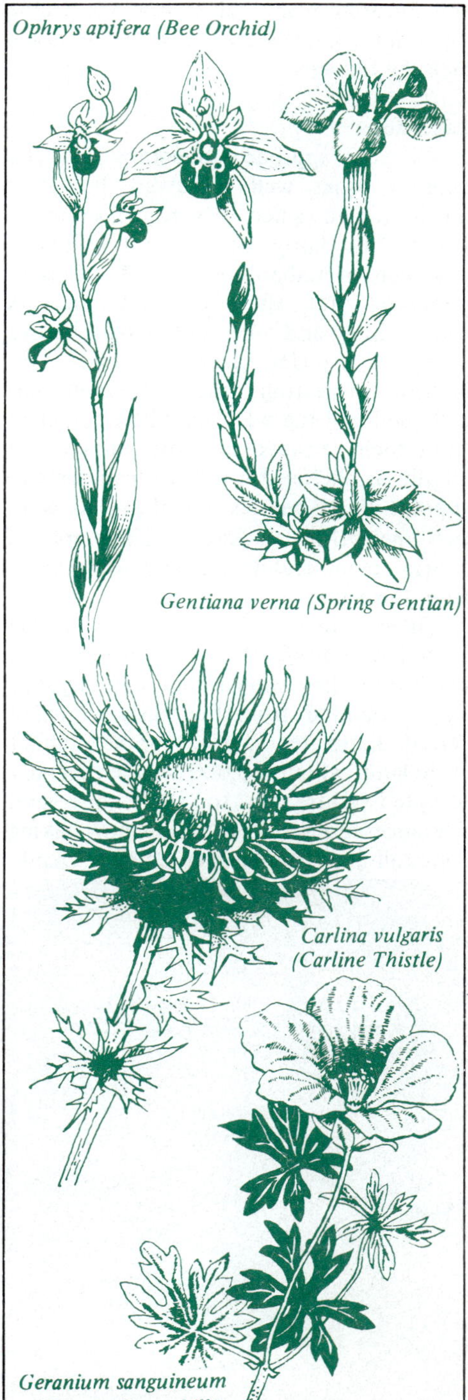

Ophrys apifera (Bee Orchid)

Gentiana verna (Spring Gentian)

Carlina vulgaris (Carline Thistle)

Geranium sanguineum (Bloody Cranesbill)

and uncaring man, realises how vulnerable this unique natural garden is. Please, don't pick the flowers.

Caherdoon

As you approach the ring fort the exterior looks well preserved, but it is much ruined since Westropp wrote in 1905: "the fairly perfect and well-built ring wall of Caherdoon . . . . . terraced ramparts, hut sites, a souterrain, six metres long and one and a half metres wide, with a side chamber." Today, on interior inspection, the souterrain has collapsed and the walls have been knocked from their terraces, in some parts to be rebuilt as shelter tops. The diameter was approx. thirty metres and the walls were two metres in thickness. There are, of course, commanding and extensive views from the walls.

These cahers or ring forts were the defended homesteads of the early settlers. Excavation has shown that the majority were inhabited from the Early Christian Period. Estimates vary as to the number in Ireland: about 30,000 was a generally accepted figure up to 1960, but land clearance and reclamation are now taking their toll at an unprecedented rate. Thankfully the Burren has escaped much of this wanton destruction, and over 500 ringforts of all types remain on the ground here.

The name, Caherdoon, is a curious reduplication: both caher and doon mean ringfort. We have other fort words used similarly such as, Lisdoonvarna, Caherlis, Rathdangan, Lismoher and Lisatunna. These words Dun (doon), rath, cathair (caher), caiseal (cashel) or lios are all interchangeable, although they had definite meanings in the past.

Caher-doon used here, has its British equivalents, Caermarthen (Caher Mari dun) or Caterthun (Cathair dun). On Inishmore, the biggest of the Aran Islands, one Dúbh Cathair or Black Fort graduated to Dun Dubh Cathair.

Souterrains

The souterrain (French word meaning underground passage) is a feature of many ring forts, but they occur, too, in isolation. Some were formed of dry stone walls and roofed with a row of lintels, while others were just hollowed out of the earth. Primarily they served a two-fold function,

Inisheer, the nearest of the Aran Islands, photographed from 3000 feet (almost 1000 metres).

defence and storage; however, it is well to remember that a simple explanation does not cover all examples.

A souterrain may be described as an artificially-built cave. When conspicuous, it is generally defined as 'cave' on the Ordnance Survey maps. The souterrain here at Caherdoon probably gave its name to Ballynahown – Baile na h-Uamha, the townland of the souterrain. There is also one in Cahernagrian in the valley at the south face of the cliff.

Labhanaheanbo (Leaba na haon Bho – the bed of the one cow) is a natural cave, south west of Caherdoon. This is the legendary hiding place of the Ulsterman who will eventually lead Ireland in the final battle. In the last century some cahers with Souterrains were called ooans (a corruption of the Irish word for caves) by the local people. Another small cave near Doonaunmore was named, Ooanaleesagh, called after the Lysaght family who lived in the valley.

The Wedge Tombs

The four wedge tombs on Ballynahown were all missed by the Ordnance Survey, and Westropp found only two; but the Megalithic Survey of Clare by De Valera and O Nuallain gives full details of the four. Three are so ruinous as to escape detection easily, but it is difficult to miss the fourth well-preserved and quite prominent example. These wedges are locally called the Giant's Grave or 'labba', Diarmuid and Grainne's bed – the reputed resting place of those two as they fled from Grainne's husband, the legendary Fionn Mac Cumhail. One story tells how Diarmuid put sea-weed on the cover of the labba (the capstone) while both slept under its shelter. Fionn on learning of this sea-weed by biting his prophetic thumb imagined they were drowned and abandoned the pursuit.

This type of megalithic tomb is dated to 2000 B.C. and later, the end of the Neolithic and Early Bronze Age. The box-like appearance of the tombs due to the limestone slabs, belies their characteristic features. They all have a wedge-shaped ground plan, sloping roof and western orientation. Most of the tombs are to-day devoid of their cairn covering, and the grave goods, in most instances, have vanished. The tombs occur on pasture land, which is considerable here at Ballynahown. It is thought that the prehistoric builders were settlers from Brittany who were attracted to this place by the all-year-round grazing. Again, without excavation it is impossible to tell the burial rite, but both inhumation and cremation were practised and each tomb contained multiple burials.

Ballynahown South wedge tomb.

To visit the other wedge tombs walk south for another 500 m. from Caherdoon. One monument has only one large slab in situ, but the remains of a mound are noticeable; fifty metres south of this, in the same field, there is another ruined tomb, with the stone on the northern side standing, and a stone fence crossing the southern end of the mound.

Ballynahown South is situated 400

metres south-east of these (about 600 metres west of the last house on the road and not too far from the inland cliffs). This is the best preserved tomb, with the sides and backstone in situ, fitted into the grikes, and the smooth limestone clints used as a floor. But the roof slab is now out of position, as a result of tilting by the sides. As is the case in all wedge types, it decreases regularly in height and width from west to east. Low terracing shades the tomb to the north, but it does command extensive views to the south and west.

Time now to return to the road. The ground between here and the house is not easily traversed: high shaky walls (always replace stones) and hidden crevices add to the difficulties. It is longer, but easier, to return by going north for a few hundred metres, and then walking across the visible pavements to the road.

The road to Fanore

When you arrive back at Ballinalackan check your mileage. The road now winds down through hazel-covered limestone to the seashore, with the flora of the roadside indicating that we have left the shale behind. Ballyryan and Oughtdarra are to your right and you can see at a glance the cover and habitat provided for the fauna. As we near the sea the growth becomes sparse.

South, to your left, a limestone neck of rock stretches down by the coast to Doolin. The roadside fences peter out and you are left with rock, sea and your imagination. Although seemingly bare, this is by no means barren land. Man has lived in the Burren continuously for over 5000 years and has left, in his tombs and habitations, traces of these various settlements.

Poulsallagh

As the road turns to run parallel with the sea, we are at Poulsallagh (Poll Salach, the dirty hole – referring to the foul bottom). Here, in miniature, one may see caves, sea-stacks, coves or headlands, all formed by the ceaseless waves. The 'hole' in the name, Poll Salach, refers to the turbulent spot where an underground river enters the sea; at least the scalloping indicated waterflow outwards to the sea. But, as it has its base permanently below tide level, it is not possible to be sure. The cave does point to a lower sea level, and so is evidence of a rise in the sea level of post-glacial times.

This is a favourite spot for picnics, but please be careful with small children. Notwithstanding the foul bottom there is good shore and rock fishing – spinning, float and bottom fishing – for mackerel, garfish, wrasse, pollock, dogfish, tope and occasionally porbeagle shark and bass.

Two and the four tenths miles (3.8 km) from Ballinalackan, the road runs by periodic graffiti displays of patriotic whitewash. A helipad was recently constructed on the other side of the road for a motion picture. The erratic a half mile further on, is called an Cloch Scoilthe – the burst stone. Not far inland from here are the remains we visited at Ballynahown. A superb vista now stretches before you: terraced hills, appearing as fortified citadels, streak up from both the rocky shore and the golden sand.

Burren Geology

The Burren – Boireann, rocky land – is a plateau occupying over 100 sq. miles in north west Clare. Its limestone escarpment stretches from Corofin, north to Bealaclugga, west to Black Head and down to Doolin, where it dies away. Limestone, a sedimentary rock, was formed in Lower-Carboniferous times, almost 300 million years ago, and then uplifted from the sea. On top of this shale was laid down, and, of course, remains in the southern areas.

Generally in the south of Ireland the shale covers the high ground, while the limestone occupies the low ground or plain. But in the Burren, the limestone rises to heights little less than the highest point (Slieve Elva) of the shales, while the average height is much greater. The limestone is massively bedded, over 1000 metres thick in places, and is probably supported on a stable granite platform which gives the undisturbed character of the strata.

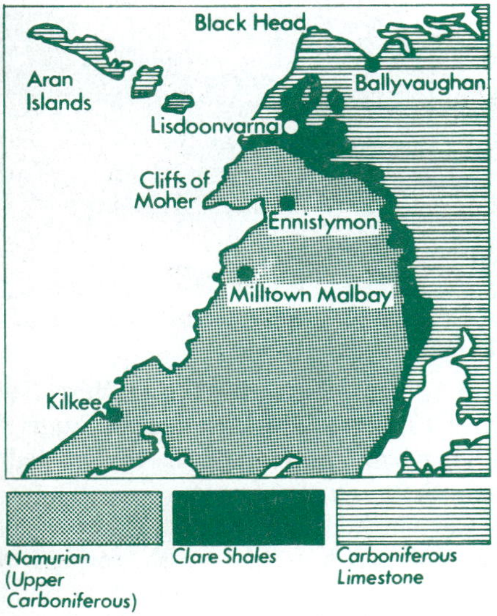

A simple geological map of West Clare.

The terracing and rock pavements, which we see today, are the result of erosion and of the scouring of successive glaciation periods: karst land, so called from a similar region in Yugoslavia. (Incidentally, the last ice age in Ireland came to an end about 10,000 years ago – some say it is still with us!) Vertical and horizontal joints occur in the limestone; the horizontal joints indicate bedding planes, the time-lapse before the next layer was formed. Terracing on the hills happened when these layers weathered away, like blocks being cut off; the hills were regular in appearance when first uplifted.

Limestone is dissolved by the solvent action of rainwater which contains traces of carbonic acid, derived from the carbon dioxide in the air. The odd shapes we see in the slabs are so fashioned because the acid seeks out the lines of weakness in the rocks. Horizontal slabs are called clints, and the vertical fissures, grikes. As weathering continues, fluting, i.e. semi-cylindrical erosion, occurs and the clints become rounded. Thin soil may have covered some areas, only to disappear from over-

The ruins of Killonaghan medieval parish church.

usage; however, most of the limestone was probably bare throughout man's presence in the region.

Crumlin

Near the shore, just before you meet the first house on the left, is a disused silver-mine, dating from very early in the 19th century. Tradition speaks of a silver-mine of the local chieftains the O'Loghlens; this mine could have been an attempt to prove the legend.

A quarter of a mile (.4km) further on, this time set against the hill is the ruined oratory at Crumlin, dedicated to St. Columba. There are eighteen different Crumlins in Ireland, including the now swallowed village in south Dublin, all meaning the same: Cromghlinn (phonetically Crumlin), curved glen. A Papal taxation document of 1302 gives the spelling, Cromglaon. No documentary evidence ascribes the place to St. Columba but, Lecknaneeve (Leac na Naomh, the saint's rock), where the saint landed from the Aran Island, is pointed out on the shore below.

The ruins are situated in a deserted farmyard, but there is not much to see. Parts of the east, south and north walls survive with seemingly early masonry; the east window, slim, round-headed and splayed, is almost identical to that at Killonaghan, two miles (3.2km) down the road. These churches appear to be of early date, but 10th century – the date usually given – seems much too early. However, here at Crumlin the presence of a souterrain across the lane in an overgrown field may indicate pre-medieval activity.

Killonaghan Church

One half mile (.8km) beyond Crumlin the hill track will bring you to the Green Road at Caherbeg. We continue north along the coast road. A small and infrequently used quay is on a little farther, followed after seven tenths of a mile (1.1km) by a restaurant and craft shop with fishing gear and boats for hire. Two miles (3.2km) from Crumlin the ruins of Killonaghan church appear to the right; again there is little of note.

The shattered cylindrical tower-house at Faunarooska.

Cill Onchon and Gleninagh, the adjoining civil parish to the north, formed the territory known as Tooflannett – Tuath Flaithnaid. Onchon/Onchus/Onchu remains an enigma. We know very little of him, except that the feast of Onchu, son of Blathmac was celebrated in July. Here at Cill Onchon you can see what is of interest from the road. The window is again, the prominent feature, and there is fine masonry of large coursed stones which have weathered to pleasant tones on the seaward side.

At the roadside there is a memorial to Garda Thomas Dowling, shot in an IRA ambush, in 1925. Then we meet the village of Graggagh, with its post office and pub (the last one before Ballyvaughan, ten miles (16km) away). East of the road, Balliny caher remains with its huts and enclosures, both inside and outside the ring wall. It was inhabited up to the beginning of this century.

Faunarooska Castle

Fairly visible, some 200 metres above sea level, is the ruined cylindrical tower-house of Faunarooska. It commands the uplands north and west of Slieve Elva, and it is also in a strategic position to dominate travel along the Green Road. Clare has three such towers and our journey takes us by them. The other two, Newtown and Doonagore, are much more interesting. However, Faunarooska is worth a short detour as its situation adds another dimension to the scenery of this coastal strip.

Take the road right, a half mile from Craggagh, past the ruins of Fanore Lodge and the Royal Irish Constabulary barracks, and continue until you are below the fortification. The castle was probably 16th century, of four storeys, built with inferior masonry, and as a natural consequence it fell seawards. As is usual, the first floor is vaulted and its lower windows are merely minute pistol loops; the inter-mural stairways followed the contours of the outer wall.

Little is recorded of the castle or of its inhabitants. It is not mentioned in the 16th century list of Clare castles. Its proprietor in 1641 however, was Fernandus Mac Felem and it was afterwards granted to James Aylmer and Henry Ivers.

If you are feeling fit continue up the hill to the Green Road, where it crosses the northern heights of Elva. One kilometre north east on the road brings you to the ridge overlooking the Caher valley, above Formoyle. A cave, 95 metres deep, the deepest in the Burren, is in the townland of Faunarooska. The entrance, is almost mid-way between the castle and the highest point of Slieve Elva (1134 feet – 345 metres).

Fanore

Back at the main road continue past the old and new primary schools to the

Sand-hills at Fanore with the Caher Valley in the background.

public recreation area, developed by Clare County Council, at Fanore Beach. It is aptly named Fanore, *Fan Oir,* the golden slope. Because of its relative remoteness from heavily populated centres it does not enjoy the fame attached to less attractive, but better-known places. All the better for those who go there. Space and solitude, sea and sand, with bathing, surfing and fishing can all be thoroughly enjoyed here.

The sand dunes are extensive and cover the limestone pavements down to the sea. North of the mouth of the Caher River is known as the Rabbit Warren where hut sites and kitchen middens (refuse heaps) of stone age man were found. A path by the north bank of the river leads to the caravan park. Shifting sands revealed a stone house by this path, some 250 metres inland. On excavating, Professor Etienne Rynne of U.C.G. could find no dating evidence.

The roots of Marram Grass, with its rush-like leaves, bind the sand grains together retaining these hills of sand. Because the sand is lacking in plant nutrients, food is sparse, but the bluish-green Sea Holly is very evident, and where there is some shelter in the hollows, orchids, especially pyramidal ones, abound. The caterpillar of the cinnabar moth is very conspicuous too, eating the poisonous ragwort – the buachallan bui, as it is commonly called. Also at Fanore there is a coastal moraine (a miscellaneous load deposited by glaciers), with scattered rocks of Connemara granite and schist.

Mesolithic Man

Fanore, Fisherstreet and Lahinch sand dunes were very early settlement sites. The evidence for this came not only from the kitchen middens, but from the artifacts

The Caher River runs through the sand dunes to Fanore beach and the sea.

found in the hut sites on these dunes. Members of Limerick Field Club were active in this area at the turn of the century; fortunately primitive tools found by them have been preserved and some are on display in Limerick Civic Museum. They include waste flakes, stone choppers, hand axes, hammerstones and a limpet hammer, all tools of our first people, mesolithic man (Middle Stone Age, 7,000 B.C. – 3,500 B.C.).

Also found here and at Fisherstreet were anvilstones and scrapers. As no site has been scientifically explored dating evidence is once again lacking. However, it is almost certain that these were the halting places of early Irish people, nomadic in nature, and living off the sea.

The Caher Valley

Return to the main road and continue to the crossroads. On the left is the main entrance to the caravan park, and right, by Fanore Catholic Church, leads into the Caher Valley. St. Patrick's Church, is a single cell building, of 1870, with a small sacristy to the east. The seven mile (11.3km) drive through the valley, to the Ballyvaughan – Lisdoonvarna road at Toomaghera, is full of interest. To keep the circular nature of this journey it is proposed to approach the valley from both ends: from Fanore we will travel as far as Formoyle and detail some of the wedge tombs, and from Toomaghera we will visit Killeany, and the forts and caves of Slieve Elva.

The Caher River

This river is the only Burren stream to remain overground from source to sea. The simple explanation given for this is that its valley is infilled with glacial drift. But in the upper valley there is no such drift, and near its mouth, the river has cut through the moraine to the limestone bed. So there must be other more complex reasons. Other Burren streams rise in the shale of Elva, to vanish underground when they reach the porous limestone, following underground the southerly dip of the rocks, south west to the sea or south east to the Shannon, via the Fergus. Steep and V shaped, the valley is of little agricultural value, as it suffers from soil creep; locally it is called the Kyber Pass.

A Cooking Place

One and the four tenth miles (2¼km) along the valley we cross the river by a simple but well-built bridge. Some 100 metres beyond the bridge, in a neck of land between road and river, and opening to the river, we meet the first of another type of field monument: a horseshoe or kidney-shaped mound, called a fulacht fiadh (roast of deer) or fulacht fian: a cooking place of the Fianna, the legendary warriors of pre-Christian Ireland.

The mound is full of burnt stones, and in its hollow, excavation would show a hearth, with a wooden trough between it and the river. Stones were heated on the hearth and dropped into the trough to boil the water, which was channelled from the river. Experiments have shown that 100 gallons (455 litres) of water could be boiled in this manner in less than half an hour. Meat – pork was the favourite – was insulated in straw, and boiled in the usual manner of about twenty minutes to the lb. (.45kg) and twenty minutes over. Or, of course, it could be roasted on the hearth. The size of the mound of burnt stones indicates the extent of usage. When we return to the coast road, a much more imposing example will be visited.

A Penal Chapel

Travel for half a mile (.8km) from the Fulacht Fiadh to beyond the next house on your right. Less than 100 metres up the hill, on your left, in a dense thicket, is a tiny crude building: a penal chapel, hidden as it always has been. It measures 3m x 4m with a small ante-room 3m x 2m; a

temporary lintel in the doorway denies access to bigger animals. A small bullaun (early mortar) and what could be an altar slab survive, with offerings from to-day's people. Add, as I did, a prayer, wish or offering to the countless others. What stories this simple building could tell! How often was it used in those dark days of religious persecution during the 17th/18th centuries? Maybe it should keep its secrets. Higher up the hill is Formoyle killeen, and nearby is the deserted village of Caherbannagh.

Formoyle

At the crossroads the main road veers right for Elva and Lisdoonvarna. Travel the very short distance, again crossing the Caher, to the ruined church of Formoyle, sited at the junction of the Green Road. Here, in 1317, O'Brien mustered his troops before going on to tackle his rivals at Corcomroe Abbey. This church preceded St. Patrick's at Fanore and was in use until 1870. The walls, with blocked-in Gothic windows, are now only seven feet (2.1 metres) high; the building may originally have been T-shaped. Lying around the ruins is a shallow broken bullaun: sometimes their presence indicates early activity on the site. You may continue on the main road to Pollnagollum and Killeany but, as I have stated, it is intended to detail these from the other side of the valley.

◀ *The Caher Valley with its road and river.*

The terraced hills overlooking the western entrance to the Caher Valley.

Caheranardurrish

Return to the crossroads and go right. Almost immediately the Green Road continues up the hill. A short stiff walk will bring you to the stone fort, Caheranardurrish, overlooking the valley. This repaired caher seems to have been in use up to recently; indeed, tradition tells that it housed both a chapel and a sheebeen (illicit drinking place, usually selling the local hard stuff). Certainly, the long rectangular building with the double door lintel does appear to have had some public use.

The name is sometimes translated the

same as the caher between Gleninsheen and Poulnabrone: Cathair an Ard-Dorais, the fort of the high door, but this meaning is unlikely here. Walk across the brow of the hill to overlook the Feenagh/Rathborney valley. The small cliff fort of Lismacsheedy is quite conspicuous across to the right, at the foot of Cappanawalla, and Feenagh ringfort is to the left. Our Green Road follows the valley into Gleninagh South and climbs the hill of that name, overlooking Galway Bay, to descend finally to the coast road.

Derrynavahagh Wedge Tomb

Of all the Burren wedges, Derrynavahagh, is one of the best preserved and one of the hardest to locate. Back down in the Caher Valley continue on the minor road for one mile (1.6km) where the tomb is about 400 metres east (left) of the road. If the cliffs appear too formidable continue on the road until you meet a non-working side gate. By climbing some 300 metres up the hill and then walking north (parallel to the road) for 400 metres, the tomb, or a nearby L wall, should be visible. But be warned: this is a difficult walk with treacherous conditions underfoot.

Derrynavahagh *(Doire na bhFathach,* the oakwood of the giants), lies on a fairly level platform, 400 feet (121 metres) above the Caher River, commanding extensive views, especially north west through the valley to the sea at Fanore, and across to Galway and the Twelve Pins. The chamber is well preserved with one massive cracked slab on the north, and is the normal wedge type, sloping and narrowing from west to east. A fraction of the original covering cairn seems to have survived. Notice the low mound south west of the tomb.

Extensive rough pasturage surrounds the monument, providing good winterage, that is, grass for winter grazing. This practice, common in the Burren hills, but in few other places in Ireland, affords the farmers some compensation for their rocky acres. Signs of recent habitation surround the tomb, possibly pointing to its use as a herd's shelter.

Half a mile (.8km) south east of Derrynavahagh, almost straight in from the roadside gate, are the two ruined Faunarooska (east) wedges, only forty metres apart. One is completely collapsed and the other almost so. Across the bog road from these are the hoof marks of the legendary Glas Ghaibhneach (Glasgeivnagh) cow, whose supply of milk was so great that no vessel could hold it, but who died of humiliation at not being able to fill a sieve! This is the same cow we met at Ballynahown. Time now to return to the sea.

Limestone pavements at Murrough near the fulachta fiadha.

Around Black Head

Return to Fanore. The first turn right after crossing the bridge leads to the old road which circles Black Head, joining the main road again at Gleninagh. It offers excellent views and provides many opportunities to examine the flora: Black Head is a remarkably rich area.

Three quarters of a mile (1.2km) from the bridge, opposite a new bungalow, there is another small fulacht fiadh: a grassy mound, about 100 metres in, on the rocks. Continue on the road for 150 metres to a lane, where we meet the sign for Fanore. Near here we will examine a more imposing cooking place. Walk down to the end of the track, turn left and, after another 100 metres you should see the fulachta fiadha, towards the sea, looking like disused quarry heaps on the edge of the pavements. A temporary stile grants easy access to the fields.

There are at least two cooking places here with the absence of water pointing to periodic usage. We cannot date these field monuments to any fixed time. Radiocarbon dating at excavated sites has shown their prehistoric use, but tradition places them in historic time, too. Geoffrey Keating's Forus Feasa (a medieval History of Ireland), describes how the Fianna cooked the meat captured during the hunt . . . how they roasted some and how it was their custom, "to bind portion of it in dry bundles and set it to boil in the larger of the two pits and keep plying them with stones that were in the fire, making them seethe often until they were cooked."

Until recently most of the known cooking places of this type, were in south Munster; now we know that at least thirty sites have survived in the Burren These are good examples here, at Murroughtoohy South. Murrough means level land along the sea, producing coarse marine grass. We have Murroughtoohy and Murrough-

The horse-shoe shaped fulacht fiadh at Murrough.

killy. As the Bishop of Kilfenora owned land here, this was known as Murrough-killy: cille, of the church. The 'toohy' represents lay Murragh, from tuatha, a layman.

Limestone Pavements

Walk on the clints and across the pavements towards the sea and notice how deep the grikes are. What community or hunters sat around that cooking place? Did soil, albeit then a thin covering, hide these rocks? Did they overgraze and so leave to us today's karstic features? How, when, where did they live? There are too many pieces missing from the archaeological puzzle to answer any of these questions.

Cathair Dhuin Irghuis

Drive on towards Black Head to our next stop, one of the highlights of this Burren journey: a walk up Ceann Boirne to the fort of Dooneerish, Caherdooneerish. This is the caher of Irghus, the legendary builder. It is haunted by him and not by Fergus, as is sometimes related. Stop short of Black Head, about two miles (3.2 km) from Fanore, where a boundary wall snakes up the hill; let this be your guide up to the caher at 650 feet (197 metres). The climb will take, at your leisure, about one hour.

The walk and the view were stimulating, but I found the caher disappointing and not in the least spectacular. It is D shaped, almost irregular, with a four metre high south-eastern wall; diameter of about twenty five metres; doorway two metres wide: some wall terracing; masonry irregular and poor, and showing signs of successive rebuildings. The caher's prominent situation hints at some ceremonial use.

On the Mountain Top

If you are feeling fit, and out for the day, why not head for the highest point: the cairn at Doughbranneen? It is 1045

The fort of Dooneerish – Cathair Dhuin Irghuis – overlooking Black Head.

feet (317 metres), on the terraced hill, one and a quarter km south east of the caher. Seefin (Sui Finn, seat of Fionn), north of Doughbranneen is another cairn, though it is nearly levelled. At Seefin, the legend tells that the intruder, Lon Mac Leefa, was finally defeated by Fionn Mac Cumhail.

These cairns are probably burial mounds, containing cist burials of the Bronze Age. An excavated cairn at Poulawack was found to contain the remains of eighteen people, only two of whom were over thirty five. Our journey will bring us to an impressive example: the marsh-cairn of Carn Connachtach, near Kilshanny. But that is in the south Burren. Right now we are on top of Gleninagh mountain, walking eastwards along its ice-polished top to Aghaglinny South townland. A most unusual, earthen, oval-shaped ringfort, seventy metres from east to west and thirty metres across, rests on the bald summit, again 317 metres above the sea. We do not know why there should be a ringfort of earth, when suitable slabs were readily available.

You may prefer to return to Black Head by a different route. The Green Road, a little further to the east, leads down to Gleninagh. If you decide to descend nearer to Black Head, be careful, for seepages occur along the bedding planes of the rocks, making them very slippy, and the cliffs are quite steep.

Black Head

The view from Caherdooneerish across Galway Bay, west to the Aran Islands, or east along the coast of County Galway, is superb. Galway Bay, the Ireland-for-distant-hearts, looks more attractive from this side, framed as it is with the Twelve Pins of Connemara in the background. Many visitors, however, feel they have not seen Galway Bay until they are on the Galway coast! It is beautiful, no matter how trite it sounds, to watch the sun go

Around Black Head and into Ballyvaughan Bay.

down on Galway Bay.

North, across the bay from the automated lighthouse on Ceann Boirne, is Spiddle; Barna is the village across from Ballyvaughan. Inland from the lighthouse, at 100 feet (30 metres) O.D., there are several tiny caves or recesses; their existence hints at an old sea level at this height. Also, particularly here at Black Head, the several coastal platforms at various heights above sea level, seem to point to the same conclusion. But no evidence, in the form of any raised beach deposits, presents itself anywhere along the coast. Erratics, with fine striae (thread or flute-like markings), are found just above the storm beach at Fisherstreet and in the moraine at sea level at Fanore. None of these markings could have withstood a period of wave action, and so their presence means that the sea level, since glacial times at least, must have been lower than it is now.

Whatever the origin of the rock shelving, it does provide natural platforms for the shore angler, fishing for dogfish, mackerel,

Gleninagh tower-house, an O'Loghlen stronghold.

Looking across Galway Bay from the automated lighthouse to Connemara.

conger, pollock and wrasse. Black Head is also an ideal place to observe sea-bird passage, as the extensive sand and mud flats of inner Ballyvaughan Bay provide resting places for those migrating. Also, brent geese from the North American Arctic spend their winter months there.

The road inland from Black Head, commanded by the scarps of Gleninagh on one side and the rocky foreshore on the other, leads south eastwards to Ballyvaughan and to other helter-skelter Burren hills in the background. Two and two tenth miles (3½km) from the lighthouse, across from a small quay, the old track from Fanore descends to road level. Gleninagh castle, our next stop, should be visible on the foreshore ahead.

Gleninagh

The turn-off for Gleninagh Castle *(Gleann Eidhneach,* ivy glen) is a little over three miles (4.8km) from Black Head; you may drive down. This concentration of castle, church, well and well-house, fulacht fiadh, limekiln and ruined houses provide excellent illustrations of medieval archaeology.

Inside the gate, at the end of the lane, to the left, is ruined Gleninagh Lodge. This and Fanore Lodge are the only two domestic buildings of any note in this north Burren corner. Notice the huge, cracked fireplace lintel and the graveslab of 1650, with a cross and an undecipherable name, inserted near the chimney top.

To the left, in front of the castle, is Tobernacrobaneede *(Tobar na Croise Naoimhe),* the holy well dedicated to the Holy Cross, with its 16th century well-house and enclosure with seats. Most of Gleninagh was owned by the See of Kilfenora in the mid 16th century; this could account for the elaborate well-house and its dedication.

The 16th century tower-house was an O'Loghlen stronghold which they inhabited until about 1840. As has been

The holy well dedicated to the Holy Cross at Gleninagh.

mentioned, the O'Loghlens were Princes of Burren. Unlike the O'Connors of Corcomroe, they retained their tuath. As is common in these L-shaped castles, the spiral staircase is in the smaller projection. The built-up approach is unusual, maybe allowing for a later doorway. Notice how well protected it is, with a menacing machicolation, itself fortified with musket holes. The first floor is gone, but the second has a vaulted ceiling.

Recently the Commissioners of Public Works (OPW) carried out conservation work at the castle. Protruding pieces of polythene show this repair work on the masonry, windows and fireplace! Bartizans defend the two corners nearest the sea; notice the garderobe opening in the north-east corner and the hood moulds over the windows.

Looking across to the mountain from the door of the castle, over the well-house, you should see the track of the Green Road (this is definitely the last mention of it!) on the col between Gleninagh and Cappanawalla mountain. It winds down to join the road, ½ km back towards Black Head.

East of the castle, the cooking place is very prominent; could the stone trough (?) some metres away, be connected with its function? Nearby Gleninagh medieval parish church is ivy-covered – you can see it, to the right of the lane, on your way back to the road. Notice, also on the other side of the lane, a small ringfort, divided by the field fence. And, if you have not your fill of fulacht fiadh, another one is sited across the road at the junction.

Gleninagh is an Irish speaking area, principally because of its contacts with Connemara, but sadly, only three native speakers remain. The main trade was with the hookers, bringing turf and poteen across the bay.

To Ballyvaughan and its Valley

The Pinnacle Well

The Burren is really a land of wells, holy or otherwise, mostly with the prefix, 'Tobar', the Irish word for well. Not many are as decorative as Tobercornan, the Pinnacle Well, which now invites you to stop shortly after leaving the Gleninagh lane. Tobar Chornain, the old name of the early 19th century Gothic stone structure, with diagonal buttresses and capped with its stumpy pinnacles, is puzzling: was it named after a person Cornan or is it the Irish word for a plant name, Cornan?

The well-house hides access to the water rising behind through two U-shaped channels in the limestone. As this was the main water supply for Ballyvaughan village in times of drought, the well-house may have been deemed necessary. Also, as it is a perennial well, the house may have saved the road from erosion, although there is now no evidence that the water flowed across the road. Interesting also that the volume seems to change little from season to season. Say a silent prayer for the people who paused to decorate our journey with this stone canopied well-house. Will our generation ensure its survival?

Cappanawalla

As we continue towards Ballyvaughan, Cappanawalla mountain provides the rocky side drop, and the foreshore at low tide exposes mud flats and seaweed-covered rocks: clusters named as Black Island and Farthing Rocks. Two miles (3.2 km) across the shallow bay the Martello Tower at Finavarra Point stretches out, still waiting to repel the threatened Napoleonic invasion of the early 19th century.

Finavarra and Aughinish Island towers guarded the southern sand banks, which were thought to be suitable landing spots for the French flat-bottomed barges.

Seaweed is collected here for use as manure (crushed shells and sand are also used). Mostly it is cut-weed or cut-wrack which grows between high and low water level. Although seaweed is used to some extent in the manufacture of ice-cream and toothpaste, certain seaweeds may have potential not now realised: a survey of Ballyvaughan Bay seaweed may show its use in skin-care seaweed cosmetics. There is certainly no shortage of it here as we prepare to enter Ballyvaughan by the road skirting the knuckle of land called the Weathercock.

Tobercornan, the Pinnacle Well. ▶

Ballyvaughan Quay

Ballyvaughan village, as we see it today grew from the early 19th century, possibly as a result of the building of a quay by the inhabitants themseves. This proved unsuitable, so the Fishery Board erected the present one in 1829; by 1841 the village had thirty five houses with 235 people. The quay was the life-line as the village looked across the bay to Galway for all its supplies; but only small steamers could ply, owing to the shallow waters.

Local exports were grain, bacon and vegetables, from the weekly markets, while turf was shipped from Connemara in great quantities on the hookers. Steamers also brought visitors from Galway. At the turn of the century, one steamer offered a sort of a package deal from Galway to Lisdoonvarna.

With improved roads and worsening pier facilities all this trade faded away. Today, both piers are used mainly for pleasure craft, and for charters to the islands. The entry to the other pier is around by the small, rocky inlet, The Goleen, *(Goilin,* means that type of inlet), and then down the road past the neat cottages.

Rent an Irish Cottage

These prominently sited cottages were built by Rent an Irish Cottage Ltd. – a company formed in the late 1960s', comprising statutory bodies and community groups, to build traditional Irish cottages for rent in the Shannonside region. While keeping many traditional features, they have all modern conveniences, and consequently have been a success story all the way as these figures from the 1978 accounts show:

"Highest occupancy figure in any

The coastal strip from the Pinnacle Well to Black Head. Notice how the castle dominates the patch of good land.

sector of the Irish Tourist industry, 68% occupancy rate for the whole year; 95% of all occupants, April to October 1978, were overseas tourists; visitors to the ninety-eight cottages sited in eleven villages, spent £1½ m. in the Mid-West Region during that year".

The cottages are extremely comfortable, and the retention of the thatch, the half-door, open hearth, dresser, loft and other subtleties of a vanishing Irish lifestyle provide an experience in living for anyone. Indeed, visiting residents find that they are tourist attractions, as busloads of other travellers try to glimpse and photograph the peasants of the day! Of the peasant dwellings of 1840, a visitor wrote: "cottages are always thatched with straw, sedges, rushes, heath or potato stalks; a want of cleanliness is universally prevalent"! But the supervisors of Rent an Irish Cottage ensure that only the highest standards of comfort and hygiene prevail.

Ballyvaughan Castle

Opposite the entrance to the cottages, on a grassy spur of land, are the foundations of Ballyvaughan Castle, another O'Loghlen stronghold, destroyed even long before 1840: "Castle of Ballyvaughan (called in old Irish manuscripts, *Baile Ui Bheachain,* i.e. O Beahan's town) stood on the brink of the bay, close to the village of the same name. It is now destroyed, and the site encroached on by the sea. A few fragments of its walls, scattered about, are the only vestiges remaining of this castle". (Ordnance Survey Letter).

It had its moment of history, though:

The Rent an Irish Cottage scheme with the castle site on the rocky promontory, and the ringfort to the rear.

Inset is a Lawrence print showing the former main street of the village.

1569 saw the first attempt to introduce Protestantism into Clare, and the Four Masters tell that Ballyvaughan was one of only two castles which resisted. Not for long, as the then Lord Deputy, Sir Henry Sydney, was marching with a considerable force, the castle was reduced with little difficulty. To little avail, for the Parliamentary Gazetteer records that in 1834 the parishioners consisted of "twenty churchmen, four Presbyterians and one thousand eight hundred and sixty three Roman Catholics; and there was neither church, chapel nor school".

When Rathborney was united with Drumcreehy (two civil parishes which comprised all the surrounding area), the present Catholic Church was built, circa 1860, and a neat Church of Ireland building was erected on the other side of the village. With admirable ecumenism when this church closed, it was taken down and re-erected as a Catholic church in Noughaval, where it was re-dedicated, in 1943.

Medieval Settlement

Before the present village grew, a late medieval settlement seems to have been centred here on this semi-promontory around the cottages: not only does the castle point to this, but Westropp in 1900, tells us that 'three small forts and a much levelled ring of a great caher lie near the quay'. This appeared on the Ordnance map as a moated rectangular site. A small ring fort survives behind the end cottages, and although the larger fort is not now discernible, the Board of Works with admirable foresight, placed a preservation order on the surrounding fields.

Ballyvaughan Village

Ballyvaughan was the administrative centre for north-west Clare having a large

Ballyvaughan looking north.

police barracks, coastguard station, workhouse and attendant Board of Guardians. We are told that difficult or obstinate officials were sent here on promotion! Tourism and fishing were the major industries: McNamara's Hotel on the shore featured in many a 19th century guidebook, and a herring fishery and thriving oyster bed were successfully worked. But even as far back as 1804, Dutton could tell that the oysters had become scarce for want of stocking the bed.

Today, tourism and fishing continue to provide the best hope for development. The fish processing plant is re-opening and oyster farming, though now worked on a small scale, must have tremendous possibilities. With its situation and surrounding attractions, the future of the village as a major tourist centre seems assured. Certainly the cottages, the development of Aillwee cave, Gregans Castle and Hylands hotels, the Merriman Winter school, the emphasis on crafts and the general upsurge of interest in the Burren, have all helped, but the population never-the-less continues to decline. The population to-day is less than 150, and Ballyvaughan as a market town is for the history, not the geography books.

Holiday homes are not the answer, for a seasonal migratory population creates its own imbalance, stretching facilities to the limit at peak season and leaving the permanent residents to virtual hibernation for the non-holiday months. Recent efforts to bring new life, notably the North Clare Vegetable Co-operative, failed: lack of management and marketing skills, yes, but most of all, sadly, lack of co-operation from the people whom it was meant to serve.

Through the Village

On the right entering the village is O'Loghlens, where the supervisor for the Irish cottages lives. To the rear of these premises were the privately-owned fair-green and weigh house. The fountain was erected in 1875! The stonemasons were

The fountain in the square at Ballyvaughan

the Coyne Brothers who came across from Connemara to Gleninagh with turf, in the mid-19th century. Their boat sank at the pier, and they went into voluntary exile here, becoming masters of stone and still!

The main Galway road to the left will lead you to such delights as Corcomroe Abbey, Ochtmama early churches and Dun Guaire Castle at Kinvara, all journeys for other days. We are heading inland by Hyland's Hotel, south for Corkscrew Hill and Lisdoonvarna. Check your mileage at the fountain.

Behind 'Guthrie victualler' is the short-lived vegetable co-op. As you round the corner the Catholic Church looms to your right, a solid nave and chancel Gothic building, with tower and spire at the north side. The drainage channel left of the road is the re-emerging Rathborney river; it discharges into the sea at Goleen.

At the junction one mile from the village, we will be travelling straight on south, following for a few miles the route of the first Burren Journey. As Newtown Castle, Rathborney and Gregans Castle are all detailed therein, I propose to give only skeletal information on them here.

The road left to Corofin is fascinating: cahers, castles, churches, wedge tombs, and the most photographed dolmen in Ireland, Poulnabrone, are all situated on the road edge. And of course, less than a mile (1.6 km) from this junction, we have the turn-off for Aillwee cave.

Aillwee Cave

A visit is a must; and for the person scared of going into the cave, the view from the car park and the facilities are ample reason for the drive to the top. The development at the cave entrance, so skilfully hidden externally, is worth travelling a long distance to see. How fortunate for the Burren that this project is being handled by sensitive environmentalists. In 1979 a further half mile (0.8 km) of cave was opened to the public, making the excursion a memorable experience. A proposal to turn the surrounding land into a wild-life park may yet come to fruition.

Newtown Castle

Some 200 metres south of the junction on the Lisdoonvarna road, the second cylindrical castle, Newtown, is noted on your right. This is in good condition and has many sophisticated features. Originally built in the 16th century as an O'Brien tower, it was inhabited in 1839 by Charles O'Loghlen, Prince of Burren. Newtown rises five storeys high, from a square – almost pyramidal – base, into a round

The entrance to Aillwee cave belies the interior development.

tower, from the top of which there are good views. This is a most important fortification, strategically sited on the edge of the bare limestone, commanding the valley.

One and six tenth miles (2.6 km) from Ballyvaughan on the left, are the house ruins of Dr. P. J. Kelly, a well known Burren botanist, and the remains of his garden.

Turloughs

If you are making this journey in wet weather or in wintertime, you may see small lakes, or flooding, in the fields, as you travel through the valley. These are turloughs, temporary lakes, a common sight in the Burren, when the water table rises. In the summer the rocks are covered with the white papery remains of dead algae.

Rathborney Valley

Two miles (3.2 km) from Ballyvaughan, a detour to the right on the tarred road leads through Rathborney into the fertile Feenagh Valley, on the Southern slopes of Gleninagh and Cappanawalla. Rathborney medieval parish church (the old civil or pre-Reformation parishes of Rathborney, Drumcreehy, Killonaghan and Gleninagh make up the modern parish of Ballyvaughan) is sited in an earthen ringfort, about one kilometre down the road; it has some interesting features. Many cahers dot the valley. Here too, Rathborney stream will disappear into a sink hole east of the main road, and remain submerged until, as we saw, it reaches the village.

Gregans Castle

We meet Gregans Castle at three and three tenth miles (5.3 km) from the fountain. The hotel, although dominating the foot of the hill, blends in pleasantly. There are in fact, three Gregans castles. The original tower-house is across the road from the hotel beside the unfinished (?)

Rear view of Newtown Castle.

17th century strong-house of the Cromwellian grantee, George Oge Martyn, and the hotel was the 19th-century residence of that family. The low 16th century tower-house was one of the principal residences of O'Loghlen. Indeed, up to the end of the 16th century, Burren was known as the Barony of Gregans. The hotel now ensures that the name lives on.

Corkscrew Hill

Shortly afterwards we start climbing Corkscrew hill. As you ascend the zigzag road, the view behind unfolds: bush valley, corralled by terraced, stony hills, with a backdrop of tiny houses, sea and sand, dotted by such landmarks as the church spire, Newtown Castle and the Martello Tower. Stop at the top and ponder one of Ireland's finest landscapes.

Doonyvardan

Five miles (8 km) from Ballyvaughan the closed national school at Doonyvardan is a lasting reminder of the declining population. Since Ballinalackan we have travelled through the electoral areas of Derreen, Slieve Elva, Gleninagh, Drumcreehy and Rathborney. The total population of these areas in 1911 was 1,540, which by 1971 had dropped to 819, a 47% decrease in sixty years. The 1979 census returns show that the decline continues, and the population density is now less than fifty people to the square mile.

Although there are pockets of good land by the coast and in the Ballyvaughan Valley, the soils are deceptive and poor. Farming, then, is hindered both by thin, boulder-covered soil and by the high number of fragmented farms. An average of one hundred and twenty acres (48 hectares) is needed to make an unsubsidised living, But only 50% of the farms have twenty acres (8 hectares) or more.

Kilfenora to the left is well signposted; this, the route of the first Burren Journey, travels by Noughaval and Ballykinvarga, while we take the Lisdoonvarna road.

Corkscrew Hill.

Down the grassy lane to the right is a holy bush of St. Brigid.

Gregans Wood

As the limestone gives way once again to the shale, Coill na nGragain – Gregans Wood, draws the curtain on one's view. On the peaty soil these state plantations, all part of Ballyvaughan Forest, have achieved a high growth rate. Afforestation does seem an economic solution, but it denies human settlement. A balance between the two must be retained. Planting started in 1959, and by 1974 over 2,860 acres (1145 hectares) had been covered.

With conifers making up 98%, the remaining 2% consists of decorative borders of broad-leaved trees: oak, ash, beech, birch and sycamore. Sitka Spruce is by far the most popular forming 60% of the entire plantations. It is followed by Pinus Contorta, forming 20% and a sprinkling of Scots Pine, Douglas Fir and Japanese, Corsican and European Larch. The new forestry roads and the picnic areas are definite assets, and a nature trail, common in other forests, would add much to our enjoyment of the flora and fauna.

Killeany and Slieve Elva

The road to the right, almost eight miles (12.9 km) from Ballyvaughan, leads back to the sea through the Caher Valley, skirting the eastern slopes of Slieve Elva. Three tenths of a mile (0.5 km) down the road a gravelled track leads part of the way to Killeany ruined parish church, which you can see, seemingly isolated in the fields. In wet weather, as the water table rises, access to the church from this side is difficult; entry then is down a lane from the main road.

Hydrology

The gravelled track ends abruptly at a swallet or sink hole – locally called a slugga. Owenterbolea, the Killeany stream, is this quarter-mile-long (0.4km) 'river' which rises near the church and sinks here, and, also at the bridge. This happens because the surface intersects the water table to give these risings and sinks. In wet weather the water rises further up the valley, makes a sizable river at Killeany, and continues overground to St. Brendan's Well, east of Lisdoonvarna. This is where it normally emerges in dry weather from its underground passage. At St. Brendan's it joins other waters to make the Gowlaun River. But there is enormous variation in flow; in extremely wet weather the road at Killeany is sometimes impassible, and even the main road can be flooded.

Killeany Church

In dry weather, if you follow the stream to the pump house, the pavements provide a natural bridge across to the church site. *Cill Einne,* the church of Eanna or Enda, (a patron of Aran), is a nave and chancel building of mainly 15th century work. Lancet-type windows adorn the south and east walls, giving very little light; on the east gable, the window is well fitted, with a snake knot on the outside. The doorway in the south wall has the remnants of a Tudor arch, while the chancel arch, 3½ metres wide x 5 metres high, is made of curved, limestone slabs.

One interior slab has the O'Brien coat of arms. The explanation for this is that Cahercloggaun Castle slipped out of O'Loghlen hands and was held in 1626 by Terence O'Brien of Ballinalackan. Other decorated stone fragments, including a bullaun or font, are gathered at the altar; and in the graveyard, a cuboid of rock is also pointed out as an altar, with rounded stones on top, which are reputed to have cursing power. Aerial photography shows an irregular field wall around the church,

possibly suggesting an earlier enclosure.

Cahercloggaun

After leaving Killeany, continue towards Elva. Opposite the two storey house is Cahercloggaun, a 15th century O'Loghlen castle, built in the south corner of the caher. All that remains now is a narrow, lintelled porch still visible in the mound of rubble. 'Kaercloghan' appears on a 1560 map, and from the State Papers we glean a little of the turbulent history of that time. In 1570 Brian O'Loghlen, of this place, needed a pardon; the next year, Donogh, needed another. And in 1585 a large group of its inmates received pardon,

◀*The ruins of Killeany medieval church as seen from across the flooded quarter-mile long 'river'.*

The ringfort at Cahercloggaun showing the castle ruins in the south corner.

Donogh appearing again with his tenants or retainers, Edmond and Owen Mac Swyny, Teige Mac Brien and Teige O'Tierney. (Westropp).

The walls on the south western corner of the caher are massive, with huge regular blocks creating upright joints a few feet apart. The walls are battered, and are up to three metres wide in places. The modern insensitive contribution of two E.S.B. poles placed inside the fort, is matched by the concrete reservoir further on. Basic planning should have ensured the by-passing of the fort by the E.S.B.; and a limestone facing would make such a difference to the other eyesore.

Elva and Its Caves

Beyond the reservoir, Cahermoyle, lowered but showing traces of good masonry, is to the right. However, it is Elva with its few frightened trees, which now draws our attention. Legends tell that this mountain was the scene of seven battles fought in the 3rd century by the High King, Cormac Mac Airt.

One and a half miles (2.4 km) from the main road a pathway leads to the bog on the mountain top. At 1134 feet (345 km), shale covered Elva is the highest mountain in the Burren, rising slightly above the limestone tops of Gleninagh and Cappanawalla. Cut open far below the surface it would 'reveal a swiss cheese-like pattern, with all its caverns and caves', for there is no surface drainage on the limestone from below the shale edge. Here the road acts almost like a geological zipper, with the shale to the left and the limestone on the right. The potholes into the caves are not far away.

The principal system – the longest in the country – is formed by the Poulnagollum – Poulelva caves, which between them have over seven and a quarter miles (11.7 km) of charted passage-ways. Only experienced potholers with full gear should attempt to explore these underground rivers. Poulelva pothole is to the right of the road, a half mile (0.8 km) from the mountain track, and Poulnagollum is signposted a mile further on towards Fanore.

More Wedge Tombs

There are three wedge tombs, in varying degrees of preservation, on this side of the valley: Cooleabeg, Cooleamore and Caherbullog, all of which are difficult to locate. Cooleamore, called Diarmuid and Grainne's bed, lies on the opposite side of the valley from Poulelva, and is the best preserved. Ruined Cooleabeg, north of Poulelva, is 220 metres east of the road amid good rough grazing, which contrasts with the poor conditions across on the shale. Caherbullog, almost completely collapsed, is about a mile from Poulnagollum, near the valley floor of the Caher river.

Caherbullog House, just south of Poulnagollum pothole, has an inscription on the right gate-pier, telling that land improvements – famine relief schemes of subsoiling and drainage – were carried out at Slieve Elva in 1848.

Toomaghera

Return to the main road. The old parishes of Killeany and, our next stop, Kilmoon form the district known as Toomaghera *(Tuath Mhachaire,* land of the plain). On the height of ground, ½ km from the Killeany turnoff, we notice Kilmoon standing stone, by tradition, separating these two parishes.

Although sometimes called a cross it may well be a Bronze Age ritual pillar, de-paganised with this Christian significance. Whatever its origin, at almost four metres in height, it is hardly just a scratching post.

Toomaghera Catholic church has a 'stone built into the wall on which is delineated a crucifix in a very good style of carving'. Kilmoon or O'Grady's crossroads, scene of many a faction fight, is a little over nine miles (14½ km) from Ballyvaughan. A minor detour to the right allows us to visit Kilmoon church.

Kilmoon Church

The church and cemetery are three tenths of a mile (½ km) down the road. Like Killeany, the site has traditions of early Christian activity, but no documentary or architectural evidence. However, both churches are recorded in the Papal Taxation lists of 1302, as Kilmugown

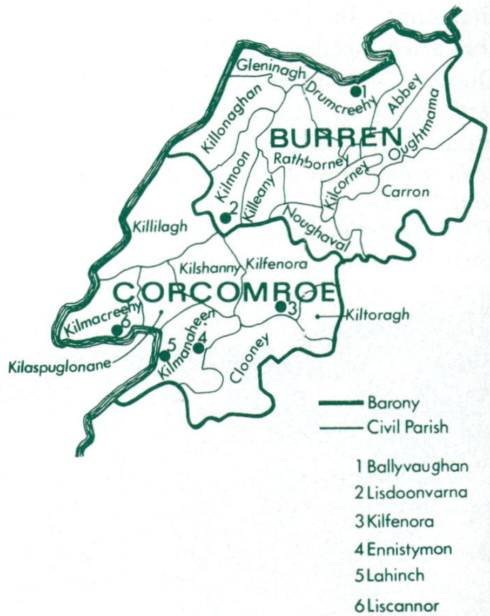

and Killeany. St. Mugain or Mugadanus is probably St. Mogua, the patron of nearby Noughaval.

The much-defaced, small church has little of interest now: two splayed rectangular windows with hood moulds of probable 15th century date, a tomb or recess built behind the altar, and another tomb-house (?) to the west. I could not find a mitred head, which is detailed for here in Westropp's writings.

Not far away to the west lies St. Mogua's well, bush and altar with another set of round 'cursing stones'. Westropp at the turn of the century could record:

It is not many years since an inhabitant of an adjoining barony beat and lamed an old woman who threatened 'to turn the stones of Kilmoon agin' him. The case was tried at the Petty sessions (forerunner of our District Courts) and it was 'proved' that, by a fast and certain prayers, going round the altar and turning the stones 'against the sun', the face of the cursed person could be twisted. And from the real belief in this method the violence of the threatened person was charitably regarded as a mere act of self defence'! So maybe you have an ulterior motive for visiting the Burren.

Kilmoon By-Road

This by-road continues to the high bogland and state forests between Elva and Knockauns, crossing four rivers all of which cut deeply into the shale. Owencloggaun sinks at Poultaloon, to re-emerge at St. Brendan's well. The Kilmoon stream continues overground – except for about 100 metres north of Lisdoonvarna – through the shale to join the Aille at the Twin Wells. The Owenealikeen sinks at Pouldonaugh. And at Blake's Bridge (about two miles from Kilmoon), in the newly planted forest, we cross over the Coolagh River, which sinks into the cave system of that name. Again, limekilns are a noticeable feature on the shale, with three to be seen on the right, within a mile of Kilmoon church. A survey of the bog was carried out in 1979. Comhar Conradh na Boirne Teo (the Co-op which runs the display centre at Kilfenora), hope to develop the bogland commercially.

On our journey we return to the crossroads; but if you want to continue the detour, veer right beyond the forest and thence to the emerald road and Faunarooska Castle. The first turn left on the untarred road, will take you over Knockaunsmountain and down to the Ballinalackan valley.

South to Kilshanny

Back at Toomaghera crossroads we follow the minor road to the left to visit the site of Lisdoonvarna Castle, a fairy mound, the remains of Judge Comyn's house, St. Brendan's Well and the Black Bridge; we then enter Lisdoonvarna from the east.

Lisdoonvarna Castle was situated beside the old bawn or terraced garden wall of a later residence, and this bawn is quite conspicuous on the right. A surviving corner-stone of a nearby house tells that the castle was built by Denis Cloghessy in 1619 for Finin Fitzpatrick. The estate passed in 1723 to the Earl of Inchiquin, and subsequent owners were O'Davorens (it seems to have been the last substantial holding of this learned family), Hogans and Stacpooles. The byroad left goes by the children's burial ground at Ballygastell.

Lissateeaun

The fort of the fairy hill, Lios an tSidheain, is on top of the prominent round hillock on the right. These shee-auns or fairy hills, with their attendant haunted stories, are very common in Ireland, particularly here in the west.

At the right hand bend are the scant remains of what was to be the Burren's finest house. Certainly, Judge Comyn's house was most unusual, as rooms, windows and chimney pieces were constantly altered in the course of construction to accommodate newly acquired furniture, doors and fireplaces. The mining judge intended to turn the place into a hotel, thereby ensuring for himself a constant stream of guests! With tremendous anticipation he moved in before the house was completed only to die shortly afterwards in 1952. Seemingly, no one else

thought much of the grand plan for the house, and demolition was its fate.

St. Brendan's Well

The untarred road to the left crosses the Aille River at Ballyteige Bridge to join the Kilfenora - Lisdoonvarna road. This is the short route to the sea that I wrote of earlier. Half a mile (0.8 km) from the house site, on the tarred road you arrive at St. Brendan's Well and the Black Bridge over the Gowlaun. Here you can see the waters from Killeany and Kilmoon rising permanently from the rock crevices. Here too, the flood stream bed has weathered through the shale down to the limestone. In time these waters will find a fault in the limestone and sink away.

Appropriately the road into town, which brings us to the square, is known as St. Brendans. Check your mileage, as once again we follow the road west, this time turning left at Kincora house. Opposite the attractive housing estate there is pedestrian access to the Twin Wells.

The Spectacle Bridge

The Aille, augmented by the Kilmoon and Gowlaun streams, is by now a sizable river flowing through a deep gorge, with 25 metre vertical sides in places. Turn left at the junction to join the main road to Ennistymon. And almost immediately you cross the Spectacle Bridge, an attractive and imaginative piece of architecture. To see it properly you will have to descend to the valley floor.

The lower part is a normal bridge with a round arch under which the river flows. But, because of the gorge depth, more height was needed to reach the road level. So a second arch carrying the road is supported by a lower inverted one, and this creates the large circular opening which gives the bridge its nickname.

We follow the inland road to Ennis-

◀ *Ominous skies cover a summer scene on the south Burren fringe.*

Spectacle Bridge at Lisdoonvarna as it appeared at the turn of the century.

tymon as we intend to visit the Cliffs of Moher from the South. This is the bog road, the bog being blanket bog of varying shallow depth, unlike the deep deposits of the midlands. Lough Goller is the small lake to the left, and on the same side, three miles (4.8 km) on, some platform ringforts are easily visible. The relatively good land attracted a number of settlers.

Kilshanny

The crossroads village of Kilshanny is about four miles from the centre of Lisdoonvarna. To the right St.Augustine's Catholic church of 1893 is of T-plan with buttresses, in a transitional style between barn-type and gothic. Half a mile (0.8 km) further on, we cross what eventually becomes the Dealagh River. West (right) Carn Connachtach should be visible, but first we will visit the abbey church of Kilshanny, almost a kilometre east.

Turn left at the crossroads and continue until you see the church, again on your left, down a very narrow lane. The foundation implies that Seanach was the founder in early Christian times, but it is traditionally ascribed to St. Cuanna whose bell, once preserved in the parish, is now in the British Museum. In 1194 Kilshanny became an offshoot of the Cistercian Abbey of Corcomroe and was dedicated to St. Augustine. Florence, its abbot, became Bishop of Kilfenora in 1273. Although in medieval records we find Kilshanny documented as one of the eight Clare abbeys, it does not seem to have survived as a monastery. In 1302 it becomes the parish church of Kilshanny. The O'Briens of nearby Smithstown Castle were Elizabethan grantees until the abbey finally passed, 'with all its appurtenances, mills and fisheries' to Robert Kinsman.

Window at Kilshanny.

Only the ruined church remains. The north door and south window are transitional, maybe co-eval with the abbey foundation, but the other features are later. Recent conservation work removed the ivy and restored the triple-light, east window. Porsoon is the townland name, It has been translated as priest's land. P.W. Joyce, an authority on placenames, states that it is simply a corruption of the English word 'portion'.

In this parish are holy wells dedicated to saints Senan, Augustine, Inghean Baoith (Toberinneeboy), and Cravans.

Stations were held at St. Cravans on the western side of the Ennistymon - Kilfenora road. Kilshanny is the birthplace of the Irish scholar, Andrew Mac Curtin.

One mile downstream stands the great stone pile of Carn Connachtach, our next stop. Back at the crossroads go straight on to the first house on the right. At the rear of the house the cairn rises on the marshy ground in Ballydeely townland.

Carn Connachtach

The Carn Mic Tails of the annals and legends is a most impressive monument, eight metres high and almost one hundred metres in base diameter. Folklore tells that the cairn was the inauguration place of the chieftains of Corcomroe, and that the present name of Carn Connachtach is applied because it entombs a defeated Connacht army! The annals record a battle near here in 1573 between two warring factions of the O'Briens, with victory going to Teige, son of Conor. So the cairn has its place in history, but primarily it is most likely to be a prehistoric sepulchral monument.

By the Early Bronze Age (circa 1900 B.C.), the impressive megalithic tombs of the New Stone Age had degenerated to box-like stone structures, called cist graves. Sometimes these are found as single burials, but are more often grouped together under a mound of earth or stone, and called multiple cist graves or cemetery mounds. A much smaller cairn at Poulawack near Noughaval, excavated by the Harvard Archaeological Expedition to Ireland in 1934, was found to contain eighteen burials and Bronze Age grave goods.

It does not necessarily follow that, just because of its size, Carn Connachtach contains many graves: it may well be a prestigious or dedicatory burial – only excavation will tell. Meanwhile the legends and folklore hold sway and the spirit of Mac Tail, son of Broc, chief of Corcomroe, can rest peacefully in his imposing mausoleum.

Return to the main road to travel the three miles (4.8 km) to Ennistymon.

This distant photograph of Carn Connachtach seems to belittle its actual size.

The town of the Cascades

This is how Banim, an early 19th century novelist, described Ennistymon. It is a small market town (population 979) of considerable charm and character. As we round the corner to enter the Main Street, the 1830 Church of Ireland building dominates the view, as many Protestant churches do, 'occupying key positions breaking a monotonous vista with their vertical landscapes'. Church services are no longer held, but it is hoped that this elegant building with its octagonal

tower surmounted by pinnacles, will function as a day-care centre.

The old market house is in commercial use again, its modern transactions making the architectural features seem a little incongruous. But maybe the round-head window, alternating with a door over gable for a total of five bays was always out of place. Many of the shops retain their traditional fronts, and many have good lettering. Notice the two-storey, whitewashed house on the west side (right) set well back and low down, evidently much earlier than the rest. Turn left to walk by the convent, Mount St. Josephs, where the sisters have been educating and giving service to the community since 1824. Continue up the hill around the cattle mart to the church and graveyard.

The Church on the Hill

This gaunt ruin dominates the town and much of the surrounding countryside, its tombstones acting as modern day chevaux-de-frise and keeping everyone in the vicinity in mind of the after life. The unadorned, nave and chancel church was built in 1778. There is a simple Gothic door, three windows on the north, and an east window showing no signs of mullions or transom; the building measures 7 m x 14 m. As Ennistymon is in the old parish of Kilmanaheen, this site is sometimes erroneously pointed out as St. Mainchin's Church, which is, in fact, a little north-west of the town. The church on the hill was the Protestant church built by the Archdeacon of Kilfenora, the Rev. James

Looking down Ennistymon's main street from the Protestant church.

Kenny, who was appointed to the Union of Kilmanaheen (Kilasbuglenone, Kilmacreehy, Kililagh and Kilmoon as well as Kilmanaheen) in 1775. It is a ruin since 1830, when the new church was built.

There are some interesting graveslabs and inscriptions. Students of naval history should take special note of the Finucane vault near the east window; and how about Morgan Finucane, M.D who wrote of his 35 year old wife: 'in fond memory of the domestic virtues of Rebecca Churchill Finucane'!

The view from the graveyard is extensive: the eye travels over old and new town to the Falls Hotel, with the winding river meandering away to the Atlantic, sentried by Lahinch and Liscannor. Our next visit is across the town to the Falls, both house and river.

The Cullenagh

The Cullenagh flows into Ennistymon from the south-east. Below the falls the river becomes tidal, and as it winds its way through deceptive meadows to the sea at Dough, it is called the Inagh. Alternating horizontal flagstones and shales provide the very picturesque cascades. The Local Authority is providing circular walks from the town by the falls and the river valleys. These should prove very popular. In season there is good fishing for salmon and trout; no fees are payable but a licence, obtainable in the town, is required.

Hydro-Electric Plant

One of the river walks passes the hotel's

The church and graveyard on the hill dominate the south-east of Ennistymon.

own 40 K.V.A. hydro-electric plant, which gives about 30 kilowatts per hour of three-phase electricity. As the turbine length is divisible by three, the plant can be used to suit the water level in the river. While it has been in operation since 1959, and has always been profitable, in these energy-conscious times the plant has really come into its own. The hotelier has thoughtfully provided a peeping hole for the curious; for the more curious the plant may be viewed by appointment.

Ennistymon House

The Falls Hotel, once known as Ennistymon House, was the biggest residence in north west Clare, and what a story this castle, mansion, barracks and hotel has to tell! Built in the 18th century, the two-storey house was incorporated into an O'Brien stronghold, retaining some of the Castle fabric. However, it is also possible that the forerunner of the present Georgian house was not the castle, but a 17th-century stronghouse with high gables and chimneys.

The original castle here was built by either Donal or Turlough O'Brien in the late 16th century. Little is known of the castle's history except that, next to Dromoland Castle, this was the most important seat of the O'Briens. Following the building of the present house by Edmund O'Brien, the estate passed, through marriage, to the Finucane family and from them to the McNamaras who added the west wing to house their shooting and fishing guests. Major H. V. McNamara – known as Henry Vee – was in possession during the 'Troubles' (Irish War of Independence, mainly 1919-1922), and actively supported the old order. He died in exile in London in 1924. Shortly afterwards the building became the temporary barracks of our fledgling police force, the Garda Siochana. Francis, Henry Vee's son, returned in the 1930's and opened the house as an hotel, with alas, as often as not, non-paying guests. More about Francis when we visit Doolin.

Brendan O'Regan – later to develop Shannon Airport as a major shopping centre – took over the running of the hotel, and during World War Two, showed his entrepreneurial flair by supplying hot lunches in hay boxes to golfers at Lahinch. The present owners, the Woods', have been running the hotel since 1955.

The two-storey, seven-bay, gable-ended house was built about 1764, and the wing added in the 19th century. There is a one-bay pedimented breakfront, with fan-lighted tripartite doorway, and a lunette window in the pediment. Some interior plaster decoration of cornices and ceilings, together with some panelling, has survived. The reception room on the right has an alcove which shows the O'Brien crest, an arm embowed, brandishing a sword, in an ornamental panel (a rococo cartouche). And in the dining room, the fireplace is thought to be a Bossi. The vast country estate of former times now extends over a mere fifty acres (20 hectares) of woodlands; and the art-nouveau metalwork of the conservatory, the mature macrocarpas, the terraces and the garden paths, serve as a silent reminder of those days of the chosen few.

Some Town Notes

Brian Merriman, author of the celebrated Midnight Court, was born here circa 1749. But Ennistymon then was little more than a river crossing. The town developed at the lowest crossing point from the sea, where the bridge is now – maybe as a result of the building of the first bridge. It grew from three miserable cabins in 1775 to 120 houses in 1810, seventy of which were slated.

The narrow street near the bridge is the oldest part of the town. Here in the late 18th century, vast quantities of coarse

Ennistymon House, now the Falls Hotel by the banks of the Inagh. The Lawrence print shows the main street at the turn of the century. ▶

FALLS HOTEL

MAIN ST. ENNISTYMON. CO. CLARE.

yarn knitted stockings, at less than 10p a pair, were offered in the Saturday market; later the use of machinery in their manufacture wiped out the home trade. A far cry this from one of the town's modern industries, Larec, which supplies fuelling valves to the European Space Agency for their satellites.

The Main Street becomes the main road to Ennis, passing the crumbling fragment of Glen Castle, prominently sited on a low hill, just outside the town. We take the road to Lahinch across the Cullenagh, 'ornamented with its elegant bridge and delightful waterfall'. The Catholic church was built in 1954 to the design of Corr and McCormick (they also designed the Holy Rosary church, Ennis Road, Limerick). This is an important building as it was in the forefront of modern church development. Today it retains its attractiveness; and the quality of the work, especially on the interior, is excellent. Worth noting are the mural stations of the cross by Aongus Buckley O.P. (1955).

The Lahinch Road

Check your mileage at the church, Stubbens, the small factory on the left, manufactures high-class leather riding equipment. Six tenths of a mile (1Km) on, again to the left, you should see traces of an embankment and a raised, grass-covered road. This was the 'permanent way' of the West Clare Railway, made famous, almost immortal, by Percy French in his humourous song of the same name.

The single, narrow-gauge line from 'Ennis as far as Kilkee' through Corofin, Ennistymon, Lahinch, Miltown Malbay, Quilty and Doonbeg, with a branch to Kilrush, was opened in 1887; the first sod was cut by Charles Stewart Parnell on January 26th 1885, and it had reached Kilkee by 1892.

Percy French's song, 'Are you right there Michael,' was seen by the Railway Company as libellous, it making a laughing stock of their line, and they sued Percy. He arrived late for the hearing at Ennis, and when asked by the judge why he was late, explained that he had come by the West Clare Railway! All services were terminated on February 1st 1961, following phased withdrawals. The line is now gone; bridge ramparts dot the countryside, and modern bungalows have been built on the embankments.

The Workhouse

One mile (1.6Km) from the church, Ennistymon Hospital, formerly the workhouse and administrative centre for the Union of Kilmanaheen, is conspicuous to the left. This attractive building is built in Palladian style (central block with flanking wings). Workhouses were built, in most cases before the Famine of 1846 and the years following it, to shelter and feed the destitute. But the people, loathing both the system and the degradation involved, tried to have nothing to do with them. A Board of Guardians controlled the Union and had much the same powers as our Local Authorities have today.

On your right, the Inagh meanders through the river meadows – the corkasses, as they are called locally, a corruption of the Irish word, carcach, a marsh. Some one and a half miles (2.4Km) from the church, platform-type ringforts are prominent on hillocks of firm ground. The one nearest Lahinch is the biggest, with a fosse of up to three metres deep in places, and commanding extensive views across the bay.

Lahinch

Lahinch is one of the best known of our Irish resorts and, at a time when other holiday towns are feeling the climate of change, continues to develop. Its good

The Atlantic waves and golden beach at Lahinch. ▲

By-gone days at Lahinch with the Norwegian hotel on the south cliffs. ▶

LAHINCH.STRAND.CO.CLARE.

beach, golfing facilities, general amenities and interesting countryside have all helped. The seaside here has been very popular since George I made sea bathing fashionable and promulgated the belief that seagrass and periwinkles were good for the health. From these trends the village grew from a few miserable cabins in the 18th century to a population of over a thousand in 1835. Rough seas destroyed the sea front so frequently that there was virtually no early 19th century development until the West Clare Railway's arrival in 1887. The general public began to visit Lahinch in unheard of numbers, especially on the Sunday excursion. Shortly afterwards the formation of the golf club all but sealed this new prosperity: Lahinch was in the big time.

The village, with a permanent population of almost 500, runs parallel to the sea, with two inland streets. It is best known as a family holiday resort, with accommodation to suit all, ranging from Grade A Hotel to self-catering and camping facilities. At the beginning of this century, when the harvest was saved, farming communities from the surrounding counties headed for Lahinch, with plenty of provisions, to stay in 'sitting-rooms with two bedrooms off'. Famaire is the special word used by Clare people for these and other visitors to the seaside. 'We won't feel now till the famaires are back again', was a favourite local saying in Spring.

A Village Stroll

Stroll around the little village. South, the road leads to Moy, and to Spanish Point, of Armada fame. In 1904 a group of Norwegian businessmen built the Golf Links Hotel, which dominated these south cliffs until its destruction by fire in 1934. The Catholic church in the village centre is similar in design to Ennistymon. Although the village proper is only of 18th century growth, the area can point to continuous human settlement from prehistoric times.

Lahinch is the Irish *Leithinsi,* a half island i.e. a peninsula. The old Irish name was *Leacht Ui Chonchuir,* the burial mound of O'Connor. (O'Connor, as we saw, was the hereditary chieftain of the area.) Leithinsi was preferred, giving many phonetic variations: Lehinnsi, Lahensy, Lahenzy, Lehinch, to the now accepted form, Lahinch.

The Strand

The strand is its life's blood, this mile-long stretch of golden sand, backed by a square mile of sandhills. It is an exhilirating place for a swim or for surfing, but always obey the lifeguard and the warning notices on the sandbanks. On occasions rough seas and high tides have taken away the sea-wall and promenade. Advanced methods of marine engineering, which have been incorporated in the recent rebuilding of the breakwater wall and promenade, should end Lahinch's greatest problem and avoid further serious erosion. The local Development Association built the amenity area, which includes a heated swimming pool, multi-purpose hall, cafeteria, games room and outdoor playground. President De Valera officially opened the complex in 1966.

Go for an invigorating walk along the strand, and look across the bay to Liscannor and beyond. Soon we will be visiting the landmarks of war, Liscannor Castle; fear of war, the Castle; telegraph on Hag's Head; and the peaceful folly, O'Brien's Tower at the Cliffs of Moher. Or buy on the promenade, in twists of paper, periwinkles (small shellfish or seasnail) and dilsk. (Dillisk or Dillesk all around the coast of Ireland.) The periwinkles are eaten locally with a pin, and the dillisk can be eaten raw or added to fish or vegetable soup.

Lahinch Golf Club

The entrance to the golf club is on our way towards Liscannor and the cliffs.

There are now two 18-hole courses, and the championship course by the sea is one of the best in these islands. The course dates back to 1892, when officers of the Black Watch Regiment, then stationed in Limerick, decided to establish a branch of the Limerick club on the links land of Lahinch. Many prominent businessmen were associated with them, including the first captain, Sir Alex Shaw. Lahinch Golf Club formally came into existence on Good Friday 1893.

The original Course was mainly east of the road with some zig-zagging across to the sandhills, which were then thought much too formidable for golf. The famous sixth hole, the Dell, which was originally the fourth, seems to be the only survivor from those times. In 1907 the committee decided that the dunes west of the road would provide a stiffer challenge. It took two years to remove or tailor the dunes for fairways, tees and greens.

Dr. Allistar McKenzie, the golf architect responsible for such acknowledged masterpieces as Royal Melbourne and Augusta National, in 1927 designed the layout at Lahinch, as we know it today. Since then, some necessary alterations have been made, mainly because of erosion and blowing sand, but also because of improved golf equipment. The Dell and the fifth, the Klondyke, remain two of the better known holes, In 1895 the South of Ireland championship was inaugurated here, and it still attracts the very best golfers annually, in pursuit of the coveted title. Membership of the club has topped the 750 mark. Visitors are very welcome.

By the Sandhills

Check your mileage at the golf club entrance, opposite the military encampment of the F.C.A. We pass by the sand dunes of marram grass and yellow pansies. The flat land here was the race course, in use formerly for flapper meetings. These sandhills have provided evidence of early settlements and habitations in the form of

The sand-hills and sand castle of Dough at the river estuary. Notice the golf greens among the dunes.

kitchen middens (see Fanore). Members of the Limerick Field Club, while exploring in 1899, found in one exposed place, 'a well marked black layer, and dug out of it one or two little bits of pottery of the same kind as we got at Fanore, also broken bones and shells (chiefly limpets), and rough flakes, but nothing of exceptional interest.' Others found an anvil stone and a hammerstone. Anvil stones were used to anchor the core rock while dislodging flakes with a hammer stone.

Undoubtedly these artifacts and sites provided the bones for all fairy stories, for the dunes are reputed to be the haunt of Donn Dumhach (Dough), the Fairy King. Andrew MacCurtin addressed a poem to him in 1740, complaining of neglect by the local gentry, and asking for a job at the fairy court. Near the bridge is the sandhill Crughaneer, supposed to be especially haunted. In these dunes, in a converted ambulance, Edward Mac Lysaght, writer and scholar, spent three summers, 'the happiest days of my youth'.

Dough Castle

One kilometre from Lahinch, Dough Castle, a shattered tower-house, stands awkwardly on one wall; the other walls fell at various stages during the 19th century, the result of building upon sand, rather than the product of war. Dough is the Irish, *Dumhach,* meaning a sand-bank, and the full castle name is: *Dumhach Ui Chonchuir,* it being the principal stronghold of O'Connor.

The first reference to Caislean Dumhcha is in 1422, but it is unlikely that any of the present fragment dates back that far. It is described in 1675, as a tall battlemented tower, having several windows and a door; a large dwelling house, two storeys high with four windows, was attached to one side. Donagh O'Brien of Dough, who received 4340 acres together with the castle, manor and town of Liscannor from Charles II, is described in 1690, as a leading Gent of Clare.

O'Connor Territory

The Irish chieftains of north west Clare were O'Loghlen and O'Connor. We saw that O'Loghlen held sway in the Barony of Burren, and that south of this was O'Connor territory: the Barony of Corcomroe or *Tuath Mor Ui Chonchuir,* the great territory of O'Connor. By the end of the 16th century, all the O'Connor castles, with the possible exception of Ennistymon, were possessed by the O'Briens. However, shortly afterwards, a scribe could tell that even this 'passed to a branch of the O'Briens, and the O'Connors have been left without a single sod of any kind of property, and there is not one of the name now in the Barony of Corcomroe above the rank of a peasant.'

The end of the 16th century saw O'Brien with full authority over these lands. Sir Turlough O'Brien, appointed to the office of Seneschall of the two baronies, was charged in 1575 'to persecute, invade, chase away, banish, withstand, punish, correct by all manners of ways and means all malefactors, their servants, followers, adherents which are or shall be malefactors, rebels, vaccabounds, rimmors, Irish harpers, idell men and women, and all such unprofitable men and women etc. All to assist.' It must have been an interesting time at the sand castle of Dough.

O'Brien's Bridge

The bridge over the river estuary is named after Cornelius O'Brien, the mid 19th century M.P. for Clare, who suggested and promoted the work. However it was at the expense of the County and of the Commissioners of Public Works that the bridge was erected. When completed in 1836, it afforded welcome relief from the ford down river – the upright marker still shows the way across. Formerly two pillarstones marked the line of the ford. Here a priest and his clerk met their death when they misjudged the way across. Ever since the spot is called the Island of Prey. The three-arch bridge, with its embankment and smaller arches, is 507 feet (154 metres) in length, and cost £4,200 to complete. Masons from nearby Clahane built the bridge,and executed many other notable works in these parts, mainly for O'Brien. As you cross, you are indeed entering Corney O'Brien Country.

The bridge spans the estuaries of the Inagh and Deelagh rivers. This Deelagh is also called the Dael, Lickeen, Ballingaddy or Ballydeely River. Thus it can claim to be Ireland's most named river. There is good fishing in the estuary waters for salmon, sea trout, grey mullet and bass. And in the bay, mackerel, herring, pollock, bass, wrasse, dogfish, conger, garfish and tope are found. Porbeagle sharks, of up to 130 lbs (58½Kgs), have been caught from the shore within a few miles of here. As you sweep left around the bend, have a good look back at the bridge: a noble piece of work of no mean proportions.

The wave-swept church at Kilmacreehy.

Killaspuglonane

When you are familiar with the country-side the following short detour or alter-native route should be of interest. Turn right three tenths of a mile (5Km) from the bridge. Straight on (left) will bring you through the high ground of Ballyfaudeen (Baile Phaidin), which was ravaged by Hugh O'Donnell's army in 1599, and then past the Doonagore Quarries to the highest point, where a panoramic view of Doolin Bay and the islands unfolds.

If you continue on the road to the right by the river, you will see a furze-covered mound of uncertain origin or purpose. Its low-lying situation adds to the puzzle: crannog (artificial lake or river dwelling), tumulus or what? We are now in the old civil parish of Killaspuglonane, Cill Easbuig Lonain, the church of Bishop Lonan. The church building is gone, but a graveyard remains. It is sometimes called gooseberry church, from a corruption of the name Killasprunane (spionan or spriunan, a gooseberry).

The Pope's own Irish Parish

Kilmacreehy

We continued along the main road to Klmacreehy and Liscannor which proudly proclaims itself to be 'The Pope's Own Irish Parish', of which more anon. Two miles (3.2Km) from the golf club a side road to the seashore leads to the ruins of Kilmacreehy, the medieval parish church. Tradition speaks of a St. Macreehy, and there is a late medieval life of Maccreiche, which however is so inaccurate and fabulous, that it is historically useless. Other than this we have nothing to suggest that here was an early Christian site, since no artifact of early date has been found in the churchyard vicinity.

Documentation from the 14th century is the earliest we have. Some of the masonry could date from then, although the decoration is much later. In the Calendar of Papal Registers for 1420, Donat Mac Machunna, is listed as priest of Kyllmeichchrichenatraga (the ending, – na traga, means of the strand), an apt description of this storm-worn, nave and chancel seaside church.

As you approach the ruin from the lane, the old masonry is visible in the lower

Kilmacreehy Church

1-7 The North Recess. 2 East Window. 3 Restoration of South Recess. 4 A Fragment. 5-6-8 Fragments of South Recess. 9 Windele's copy of Tomb.

parts of the walls. The graveyard seems overcrowded and is certainly overgrown, and the rippled flagstones of Moher are everywhere. A small porch, probably 16th-century, with a neat door and window, projects from the south wall (nearest the shore) and leads into the nave.

There is little to note in the nave: a holy water font, beside the door, one window and a broken bell chamber on the west wall. A high, semi-gothic arch separates the nave from the rather long chancel, where a break in the south wall indicates that it may be a later extension. The recess on the north wall is reputed to be a tomb, probably copying the similar monument at Kilfenora. It is a double-ogee cusped recess with a large quarterfoil opening overhead, bordered by a prominent hood which has a mitred head above the keystone position. The ends of the hood are decorated with other curious heads.

The monument on the opposite side, thought by some to have been a window, was reconstructed on paper by Westropp. It had two gothic arches, or fluted or

The wall-tomb on the north wall at Kilmacreehy.

corded pilasters, with further branching from the central shaft. A carved head with flat medieval head-dress topped the pointed hood, which terminated here with serpents of a different style: the head of a snake holding a bar or a long-necked dog biting a bone. The splayed, two-light east window has a slot on the mullion for either a temporary transom or shutter bolts. Externally it has a rectangular hood mould with floral decorations.

The ruined wall-tomb and carved head.

In the graveyard are Liddy and Lysaght vaults. A small, castellated projection on the seaward side is locally said – tongue in cheek – to be the burial place of washed-up bodies. As their identities and religious beliefs remain unknown, it was thought best to leave them half in and half out of consecrated ground!

Buried here also, in an unmarked grave, is Hugh MacCurtain (1680-1755) who, after service with Clare's Regiment in France and Ireland, became a schoolmaster and a noted antiquarian and writer. The rocks out from the shore are called

St. MacCrithe's Bed. The saint's well, with its cure for sore eyes, lay to the north west of the church. His feast day was celebrated on Garland Sunday, to coincide with the other local festivities.

A French writer could not imagine better fortune than to have been born in the area, and . . . 'to rest among the immemorial graves in the ruined church of Liscannor, to be lulled to eternal sleep by the familiar waves'. Noble sentiments indeed, but may I, eighty years after Westropp, deplore with him the lamentable state of this historic and interesting spot, and reiterate his suggestion that the southern monument be re-erected and a plaque affixed in honour of Hugh Mac Curtin.

Liscannor Harbour

This little fishing village, like Lahinch and Ennistymon, is of late 18th century origin. It grew rapidly and by 1814 it contained nearly 200 houses, ten of them slated, and about forty inhabited by fishermen. Its situation has made it a place of strategic naval importance. Ships of the Spanish Armada sought aid in the bay. The neighbouring cliffs were fortified to warn of invasion, not only during Napolenic times, but also during the two World wars. And, as if to crown the naval connection, John Holland, designer of the first United States Submarine was born in the village in 1841.

Stop at the quay and walk around. Liscannor (Lios Ceannuir, probably meaning O'Connor's fort) was named from the fort which was sited here. There is no trace today of the fort, nor of the busy port of the early 1900s when Liscannor and Moher flagstones were exported on the S.S. Clare and other steamships. Cement and politics ended that. Almost forgotten too are the curraghs, so long a part of the western seaboard, and now destined to become obsolete.

The first quay, built about 1800, was described as 'a monument to the meanness of Parliament and the ignorance of the builder'. Cut-backs in government spending curtailed the plans, drawn up in 1836, for a sizeable quay, and resulted in the irregular, polygonal quay we see today. Notice the Holland Commemorative Stone, a tribute from the Submarine Veterans of the U.S. Navy, on the east side near the road. Also, the new community centre is named in Holland's honour, and it is hoped to incorporate a naval museum therein.

The Clare Curraghs

Dotted around the coast are the curraghs which are still used extensively on

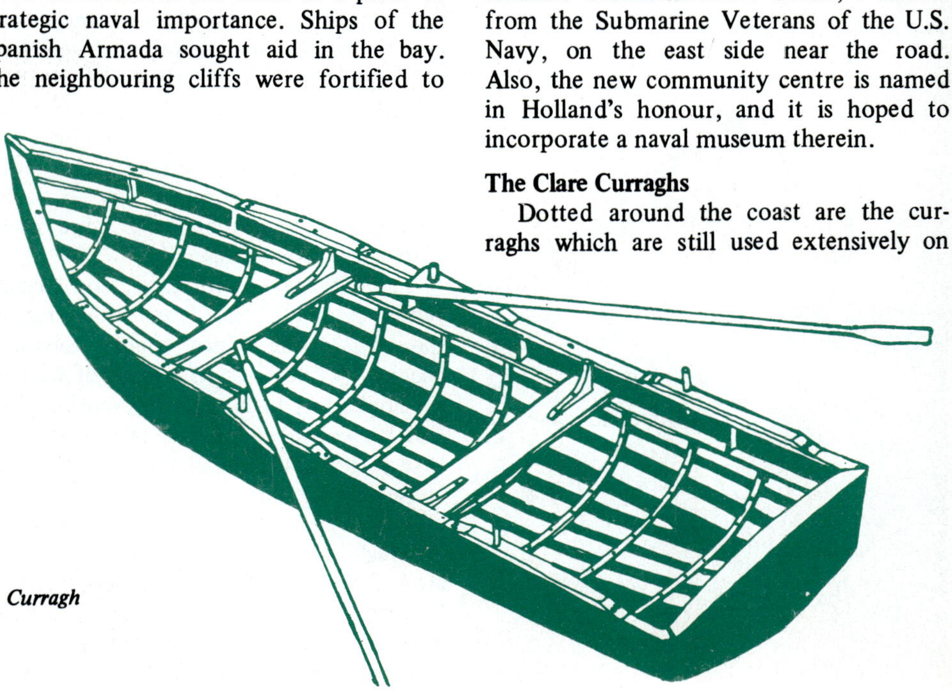

A Curragh

the Aran islands and infrequently here, and at Doolin. They are eminently suitable for the prevailing Atlantic conditions, and for unimproved landing places: strong, flexible and light, a man's load with an ancestry going back thousands of years.

But the light, canvas-covered craft with the long bladeless oars, is only paralleled outside Ireland in Portugal and Madeira. The canvas is tacked in position over the oak laths and, when the right shape is achieved, it is given two coats of boiling tar. With its long, rising prow and keelless bottom, the curragh is ideal for heavy seas. The main 19th century use was fishing and smuggling: this coast maintained great trade in sheep fleeces in exchange for wine, spirits, tobacco, tea and fabrics.

Liscannor Village

The Catholic church is a traditional, single cell of four bays, built of rubble masonry. Maurice Craig describes it and other 19th century churches as barn style, not in any derogratory sense, but to convey their simplicity . . . 'they bear testimony to proud communities and to the natural craft of their builders.'

Recent renovations added a new roof but wisely retained the gallery, the original Y-mullioned windows and attractive, semi-Tudor, inside door. Too often churches

Liscannor with its castle on the extreme left.

have been gutted in recent years and high class workmanship replaced with phony, synthetic substitutes.

A proposal to build a Round Tower beside the church in 1920 does not seem to have materialised. This Touheran tower (Touheran was the old name of the district; Liscannor Bay is Ba Thuath Reanna in Irish) was to function not only as a belfry, but its other three storeys were to house cottage industries. It was also suggested, with no little venom, that just as the towers of old were places of refuge against the Vikings, so too could the Touheran tower be used as a place of security against the Black and Tans. The money was collected, the tower was designed, and the parishioners were ready with their free labour, but the grand plan was never executed. Why, I could not discover. As another aside on the village during the 'Troubles', I saw it recorded that the barracks burned itself out of existence at that time!

The Pope's Own Parish

Liscannor regards itself as the Pope's own parish. A booklet written in 1920, and so named, gave widespread publicity to this claim. The parish is situated in the Diocese of Kilfenora, of which the Catholic Bishop of Galway is only the Apostolic Administrator – the Pope himself being its Bishop. Liscannor is a mensal parish, i.e. one under the direot jurisdiction of the Bishop, and so Pope John Paul II is parish priest of Liscannor, or Kilmacreehy, to call it by its old name.

Liscannor Castle

A left turn at the church brings you through Castle Street, and to Holland's birthplace: a small cottage, with a name plate, where his father, a coastguard in Liscannor from 1831, reared his family. See the appendix for a biographical note on Holland and his achievements.

Continue up this cul de sac to St. Macreehy's National school, and to Liscannor castle, another O'Connor stronghold, which was granted to O'Brien in 1582. The threat of invasion by the ships of the Spanish Armada brought large crowds round the castle, both for protection and to prevent any landing. On the 6th of September 1585, the Sumiga lay in Coolrone to the west of the castle and attempted to buy provisions. But a hostile population, both native and foreign, ensured there was no support, and the Sumiga (or Zumiga) limped back to Spain.

The O'Briens held the castle and lands until 1712 when the Earl of Thomond let the estate to William Fitzgerald, at the annual rent of £14; it was the Fitzgeralds who developed the village as a fishing

Liscannor tower-house.

centre in the late 18th century.

Although ruinous the castle is of interest, not least because it continues to stand, defying all Atlantic storms. It is in two sections: the tall pencil-like tower of some six storeys with the spiral stairs to the east, and the now ruinous main building of lower height beside it.

At the end of the last century, Westropp could describe this western section in detail, telling that it was of five storeys and contained all the main rooms. The slender tower is also in an advanced state of decay, but, with caution, the top may be reached for yet another view of the bay. Return to the village and turn left for the cliffs.

West to Corney's Country

We leave Liscannor and continue west along the signposted road to the cliffs. Notice on your right after 500 metres, the attractive gothic gate-house, with hood moulds and bow end. Shortly afterwards the entrance to Birchfield House, the 19th century home of the local landlord, appears before you

Cornelius O'Brien, or Corney as he is better known, succeeded his father, Sir Turlough O'Brien, as Member of Parliament for Clare in the 1830's,

The signal tower at Hag's Head.

and as a Liberal in favour of Repeal of the Union, he was returned to Parliament for over twenty years, until his death in 1857. An improving landlord, 'he built everything around here, except the Cliffs of Moher', is the frequently expressed local opinion. As his handiwork dominates the landscape over the next few miles of our journey, it certainly is Corney O'Brien Country, with even the cliffs stamped with his trademark. He helped his tenants with their buildings and land drainage, even making 'presents to the women of a cloak, or of a gown, for keeping their houses clean'. He also did his best to boost the declining population.

Birchfield Estate

Bakey from nearby Clahane built the entrance to Birchfield House, which itself was a curious toy fort in the Foreign Legion or Moorish manner. The house has been demolished and a modern farmhouse built on the site, sitting incongruously among Beau Geste battlemented stables and out-houses. A most distinctive arch, with an ornamented stepped gable, gives entry into the yard.

At the next junction, one and three tenth miles (2.1Km) from Liscannor, turn left. This is an interesting peninsula, offering new views of the bay. You may travel any of the by-roads to the shore. We are turning right at the radio masts, and then left on to the untarred road, to visit Hag's Head. Continue to end of road from where a walk of 400 metres brings you to the tower.

Hag's Head

Hag's Head is a lonely spot, but a rewarding place from which to view the cliffs. Here you will seldom have company, so you may see the cliffs in their solitary splendor, as they rise from 400 feet to almost 700 feet (120 metres to 210 metres), beyond O'Brien's Tower, some five miles (8Km) distant.

Wakefield, an 1809 traveller, tells that the view from the promontory is exceedingly grand: "Nature here presents herself in her most awful form and exhibits, particularly during storms, some of the most astonishing and sublime scenes that the eye can behold . . . . . but the eye is not the only organ which is affected on this occasion: the ear is sometimes wonderfully struck by the loud roaring of the waves."

The signal tower is of late 18th century construction, built at the time of the threatened Napoleonic invasion. With its machicolations and bartizans, supported on interesting corbels, it could be a medieval tower-house. It has a fine exterior of coursed rubble, with large dressed stones as coigns, but inside the floors are all gone. The tower is built on the site of a promontory fort – *Mothar Ui Ruain,* or *Mothar Ui Ruis* (Moher, a ruined fort), after which the cliffs are named. This fort was partly defended by building a dry-stone wall across the flat-topped spur of land, on which the telegraph tower now stands.

John Lloyd, a visitor, saw the fort and its rampart: "This moher is on the summit of a very stupendous cliff, surrounded by a stone wall, part of which is up; inside of it is a green plain. This wonderful promontory, always encompassed by devouring seas and the opposite wild coast, affords a horrible, tremendous aspect, vastly more to be dreaded than accounted for!"

Usually these promontory forts are of Iron Age date, but this one could have been built much later. Dun Aenghus on Inishmore, with its chevaux-de-frise, is an outstanding example of an Iron Age fort. Surprisingly, there is nothing else of archaeological interest along the cliffs.

Legend of Hag's Head

Beyond the platform of the tower, the

◀*The majestic spread of the Cliffs of Moher from Hag's Head in the foreground to beyond O'Brien's Tower, five miles away.*

rock has assumed, 'the shape of a seated woman, the sphynx-like head looking eternally westwards to the setting sun!' So the present name, Hag's Head, is derived by translating *Ceann Cailighe* (rendered Cancally in a 16th century map). Another legend tells that the witch or hag Mal, while pursuing Cuchulainn, fell into the sea at Loop Head, and that her body was swept northwards to this place, which was therefore called Hag's Head!

Persistent tradition says that the cliffs were joined to the southern shore of the bay, and that midway stood the church of St. Scoitheen. On clear days when the sea is calm, it is said that the ruins are sometimes visible at the bottom. But, beware: 'whoever sees the domes or pinnacles of the lost town over the waves or dimly visible under the dark waters is doomed to die within a week!' Actually, Kilstopheen is a dangerous reef, so marked on the charts, at the mouth of the bay.

Derreen

Back at the main road we pass the new school and begin to climb the hill. The Regency Gothic lodge, with a bay window in each of the two gables, on your left, was St. Brigid's National School, erected by O'Brien in 1846. Birchfield estate lies below on the flat land.

Dominating the landscape is the O' Brien monument, an urn-topped, fluted Doric column, with the fulsome inscription on the plinth informing us that it was erected by public subscription to Corney:

".......as a lasting record of his public conduct and private worth......admiration of his energy ....as a tribute to his warm hearted liberality and forethought in providing for the accommodation of strangers visiting the magnificent scene-

Dun Aenghus, the Iron Age cliff-fort on Inishmore.▶

Hag's Head, Ceann Cailighe, 'the sphynx-like head looking eternally westwards to the setting sun'.

ry of this neighbourhood.......October 1853". Corney was not taking any chances with posterity: the monument was erected during his lifetime, and the public subscriptions were compulsorily collected from his tenants!

St. Brigid's Well

Across the side road from Corney's stone cylinder (is it beginning to lean?) is St. Brigid's Well, a site for the celebration of the ancient Festival of Lughnasa, and to this day a living place of prayer, pilgrimage and hope. It may have commenced as the site of a prechristian festival, celebrated to welcome in the first fruits of the harvest.

An early 19th century account tells that 'on Garland Sunday – last Sunday in July – people assemble at Lahinch. The previous Saturday they gather at St. Brigid's Well and remain there the entire night, performing their rounds and invoking the Saint over the well. When this ceremony is over they amuse themselves 'till morning by dancing and singing. The following day they travel the three miles to Lahinch to conclude the merriment with horse racing on the strand and dancing near it'.

This pattern was transferred to the well in 1839, beginning each year on Satharn Chromdubh (eve of Garland Sunday). The well was then called Dabhach Bride or Brigid's Vat; devotions were also held on February 1st, the feast day of Brigid, patroness of Ireland. As a result of a personal cure, circa 1830, which he attributed to the well waters, Corney built the well-house, not in any revivalist style, but in a traditional manner, floored and almost walled with Moher flags, and adorned with religious and secular objects carrying messages of faith, hope and gratitude.

◀*Corney O'Brien's monument.*

Above: the O'Brien vault. ▶

Below: St. Brigid's Well. ▶

Outside, the glass-cased statue of Brigid seems to supervise the attractive gardens and circular courtyard for the rounds. At the rear stands an elegant stone cross, inscribed: In hoc signo vinces (Under this sign you shall conquer), its paved surrounds worn from countless feet.

Corney is buried in the O'Brien vault in the adjoining graveyard, even in death supervising his efforts.

After turning the gentle bend to the left, a quarter of a mile (0.4 km) from St. Brigid's, another well is visible, this time of a secular nature, with what was a pretty gothic well-house decorated with the O'Brien armorials above the opening.

◀*Inside the well-house at St. Brigid's*

Inset shows the cross in the graveyard.

Flying in over O'Brien's Tower and Goat Island.

The Cliffs of Moher

The turn to the left for the cliffs creeps up, almost unnoticed. You may be surprised to find buses and many cars there, but this is the norm; rarely will you have a chance to view the cliffs on your own, unless you arrive early in the morning. I hope the day is clear, if not you have my sympathies; and the knowledgable curator at the Tower will show you transparencies of what you have missed.

The building on the right will contain toilets, a small restaurant, a shop and other facilities for visitors. It is being built with great care and attention to the environment. Local materials are used in this simple, but sophisticated amenity. Corney built on this site too:

'a range of stables and coach-houses adjacent, all of which are liberally thrown open to respectable visitors, even without the formality of an order'.

One is not prepared for the cliffs: the featureless, rolling meadowland abruptly, almost savagely, drops a sheer 650 feet (197 metres) into the Atlantic. It is breath-taking, awesome, and frightening to many, and almost impossible to describe. Other sea-cliffs, notably those in Mayo, Kerry and Donegal are much higher, but they are not as vertical.

The suggested tour here is to follow the right hand path – behind the wall – up to the Tower. Providing welcome security and assurance for many a visitor, this wall is made of large, tombstone-type slabs of varying thickness placed edge to edge. From the Tower you will have unrivalled views of the cliffs, this great wall of Thomond, as they have been called. The cliffs, to the south, to Hag's Head, stand as massive jutting bastions defying the Atlantic. The three Aran Islands, almost a stone's throw away, seem to melt together, and at other times bob in the sea like little battleships.

The sea-stack under O'Brien's Tower is a good breeding place for the birds.

O'Brien's Tower

The Gothic twin was built by Corney in 1835 to accommodate those who came prepared to dine on the spot, and to provide elevated viewing points from the roof.

Mary John Knott was a visitor to the cliffs in the Summer of 1835, when Corney was putting the finishing touches to the tower. Writing about the cliffs, she tells that Corney '...... lately began to erect a small castle on the most elevated part, to consist of two towers with furnished apartments, connected by large buildings for culinary purposes, and stables and coach houses adjoining – all for the accommodation of visitors to this stupendous scenery, who, on taking up provisions can have servants to attend, and the only return allowed by the kind-hearted owner is that they should make a remark in a book kept for the purpose, stating the manner in which they have been accommodated'.

For years the tower was ruinous and an eye-sore, but now it has been lovingly restored, accommodating innumerable visitors every year. Corney would be pleased.

The Cliff Face

North of O'Brien's Tower at Aillenasharragh, it is possible to reach the bottom of the cliffs by taking a narrow, winding path, which, it must be stressed, is very dangerous, especially in wet weather; and landslides and missiles from on top add to the danger. At the bottom there is an immense accumulation of debris: masses of grit, shale and flagstone, from the constant weathering and sea action, made easier by the great vertical joints in the cliffs.

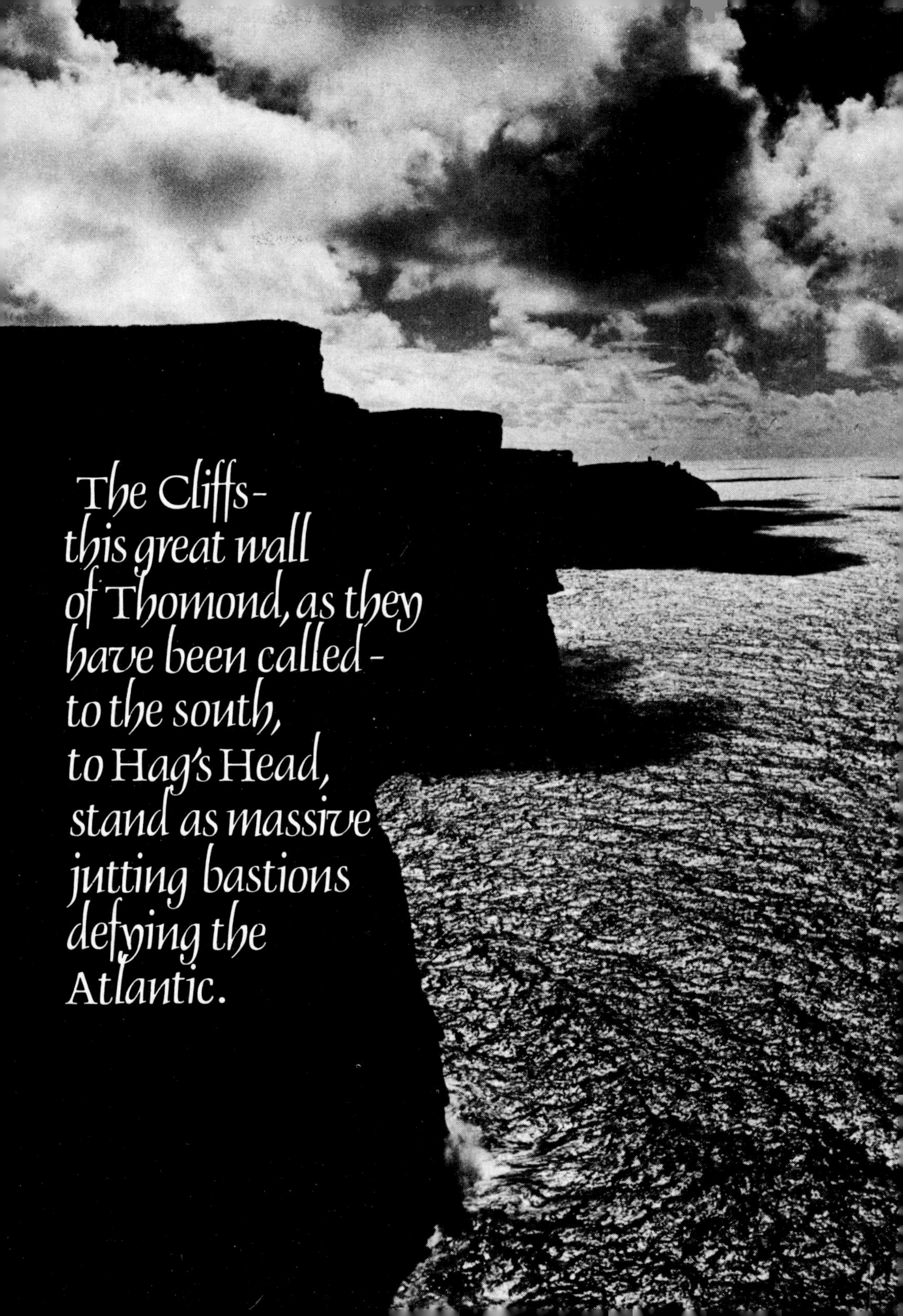
The Cliffs -
this great wall
of Thomond, as they
have been called -
to the south,
to Hag's Head,
stand as massive
jutting bastions
defying the
Atlantic.

Thin beds of sandstone and flagstone and a base of shales form the bottom of the cliffs; and then one can see the horizontal, stratified cliffs rise through hundreds of feet of flagstones to a conspicuous band of yellow sandstone. This gives the natural platform near the road. The top portion of the cliffs is composed of some twenty to forty feet (6 to 12 metres) of black shale, which was mistaken for coal by geologists of the last century. As the land slopes away from the sea, the cliffs are decreasing in altitude – on the geological time scale! From the north the cliffs are named: Aillenasharragh, Carrickatrial, Knockardakun, O'Brien's Tower on Branaunmore facing Branaunbeg, Stookeen and Hag's Head.

The Sandstone Platform

The sandstone platform overlooking the natural semi-circular amphitheatre is a good viewing place, providing everchanging scenes. A large, circular stone table, with stone seats all around, was securely fixed to the rock – some fittings may still be seen: picnic facilities – you've guessed – with Corney's compliments. Reels are sometimes danced on the platform and foolhardy, curious people crawl on hands and bellies to look down on Goat Island, and on what is usually a bird-scattered sea.

The path to the left requires a certain nimbleness of foot and a head for heights, but it does offer some of the best views of the cliffs, and of the sea-stack almost under O'Brien's Tower; it leads to Hag's Head, four miles (6.4Km) away.

The Birds of Moher

As the ledges make ideal nesting places, vast colonies of seabirds, including fulmars, shags, kittiwakes, razorbills, guillemots and puffins inhabit Moher. It was on the grass-topped sea-stack that Nicolette Devas saw and wrote of "the puffin flung from their borrows in pure joy-wheels of flight, their narrow blade wings whirring with the speed of helicopters." her book 'Two

Flamboyant Fathers' contains some descriptive pages of the bird life here . . . telling of the Nicolette call of the kittiwake, the glider fulmar and the crow witches of the bird world, the choughs, which bred in the then ruined tower. Photographs and sketches showing where the birds breed and nest on the stack are available in the restored tower.

The peregrine falcon, sadly a rare visitor – the victim of egg collectors, falconers and pollutants – was one of the great sights. Like the eagle, will it too disappear? We are told that an eyrie still existed on the cliffs in 1849, but had vanished by 1900.

Mary Knott also details bird-catching on the cliffs, but we must remember that she fell for many tall stories during her stay in Co. Clare. However, I will leave you to judge this one for yourself: The dangerous enjoyment of bird-catching is practised in the season by the hardy natives along these cliffs, for which purpose twelve or fourteen men come near the edge, and sit down in a row behind each other, holding a rope sufficiently long to reach to the bottom. One of the party ties the end of it round his body, and being provided with a basket, goes over the edge, placing his feet against the face of the rock, and holding the rope firmly, is gradually lowered by the men seated on the top, who allow the rope to pass through their hands. On the man arriving at a part of the rock where he has good footing, and within reach of the birds which frequent these cliffs in great numbers, he unties the rope, which is soon pulled up and another of the men is let down in the same way. Being furnished with a long stick, something like a fishing rod with a noose at the end, he proceeds to put it gently over the neck of one of the birds and, if he succeeds by a dexterous twitch in snaring the unsuspecting creature, he draws it into him, twists its neck, and quietly putting it into the basket, makes an easy prey of the remainder." Bird catching and egg collecting continued at the cliffs until World War Two, though hardly in the manner described above.

Story in stone of Doonagore

From the cliffs we continue north. The road bends to unfold another north Clare panorama and the three islands are once again visible. Small, disused quarries become a feature of the landscape and it is a welcome sight to see Liscannor stone being worked at the North Clare Quarry.

There are three distinctive flags: Moher flag, Hag's Head flagstone, which was quarried at Malmore, and Doonagore flagstone (commonly called Liscannor stone). Moher flag occurs all around the high cliffs and has the distinctive wriggling patterns caused by the fossil burrows of marine type worms, together with crinoid debris, nautiloids and plant stems. Liscannor stone is generally smooth-faced.

Quarrying was once a major industry on these hills, with over 500 men employed by nine companies, who worked the four major quarries at Doonagore, Caherbana, Lough and Moher. Doonagore was the largest of these and had its own

Doonagore Castle overlooking Crab Island and Inisheer.

small town, now virtually gone, except for a 'solitary shop whose keeper talks of days when sovereigns brightened her father's wooden till.'

Steam tractors hauled the slabs down to the main exporting centre at Liscannor, which up to the First World War was a busy port. For example, quarried stone went from this area to pave English streets, floor the Royal Mint and build the Redemptorist Church in Belfast. In 1904/5 Watson's quarry operated a narrow gauge railway, running for three and a half miles. Paved roads criss-crossed the hills at a time when pot-holes curtailed travel on the main roads.

Although the industry declined, masons continued to lift the slabs for walling, flooring and even roofing. As is so evident from the landscape, the stone continues to be so used, but now there is as well, quite a demand for the flags for ornamental purposes. As the writer of an article on the flags says: 'Concrete and bricks are all very fine but a man should really have a good bed of stone under him' (Jim Robson).

Three miles from the cliffs, the minor road right up the hill will take you by the Radio na Gaeltachta transmitter (broadcasting in Irish for the native-speaking Aran Islands) to Doonagore Quarry. There, the spoil heaps and chippings point to the size of the operation. Back at the cross-

OPE IN THE TOWER
AND OGEE HEADED LIGHT.
DOONAGORE

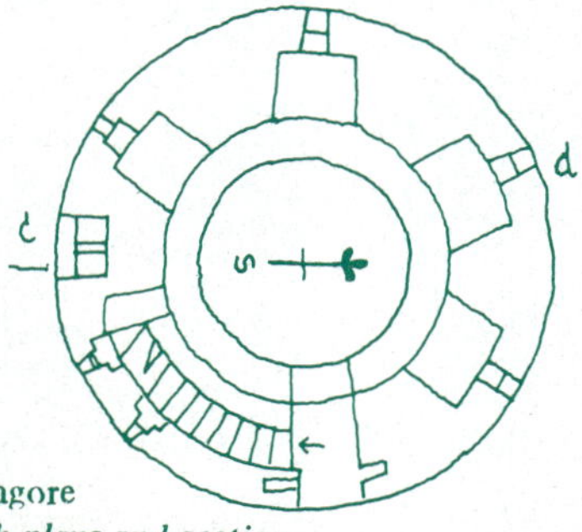

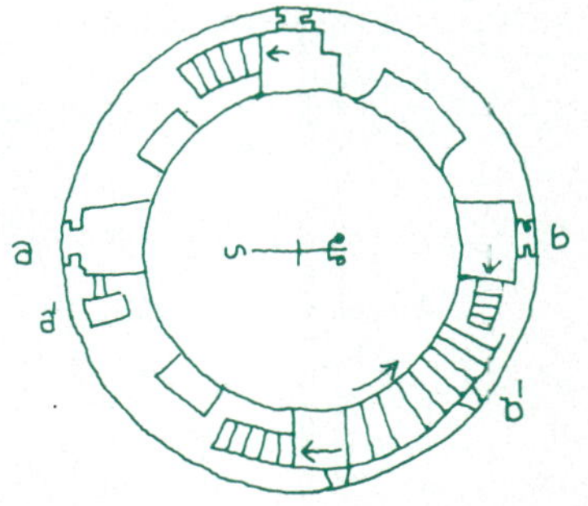

Doonagore
Sketch-plans and section

roads we are turning left down-hill, to visit Doonagore Castle.

Doonagore Castle

The fairy tale castle of Doonagore, recently restored as a private flat, smacks you in the eye as you descend to its superb site overlooking Ballaghaline Bay. As the Gores were landlords here, it is popularly believed that the place was named after them, but this is incorrect. The name comes from a now levelled ringfort lying to the east: Dun na nGabhar, the fort of the goats.

This is our third cylindrical tower-house and it seems to have a late 15th/early 16th century date. The O'Briens held it at various times, as did the Mac Clancys, the brehons. As is usual the records are sparse, but it is not unlikely that the castle was a 17th-century ruin. So it remained until the 1970's when excellent restoration work ensured that while modern comforts were installed, only techniques and materials in keeping with the original fabric were used.

The supervising architect was Percy Le Clerc, to whom we owe the restoration work at Bunratty, Ballintubber, Rothe House, Holy Cross and Graiguenamanagh. At Doonagore the restoration was so sensitively carried out that, when the castle stone was identified as coming from a now disused and worked-out quarry at Trawlackan, identical stone was searched for and located locally in various derelict buildings, and used in re-building the walls. The main work involved new battlements and roof. For this a Dinely print of 1680 showed what the castle looked like, and this is what we see today. On the top inside, the ends of shafts forming a hexagon are knit into a centre post which goes right up to the apex of the roof.

There are four storeys, each containing a main room: kitchen on ground floor, then two bedrooms, and the top floor was the Great Hall. A 16th-century window was opened here, giving an unrivalled

An Iron Age burial mound in the shadow of Doonagore Castle.

view across the bay. Full toilet facilities have been installed in the wide window embrasures, as the walls are up to 2½ metres thick, and the original shafts of the garderobes (latrines) were cleverly utilised. The (disused) discharging hole from the shaft is visible. During restoration the bawn was also repaired.

Half a mile (.8Km) from the castle, a walk along the untarred road to the left for two tenths of a mile (.3Km), and then 30 metres into the field should have you standing on another small ringbarrow. It is well defined with a metre-wide fosse, and the central mound is of the same height. This is one of many such Iron Age earthworks in this Doolin area.

Doolin

After visiting the barrow we continue to Doolin, into which our road seems to slide. Fisherstreet is the name of the little village to the left and Roadford is about a kilometre north, but Doolin is the general name.

Turn left at the bottom of the hill to visit Fisherstreet, once again crossing the Aille. This district is a mecca for traditional and folk musicians from all over the world. Indeed, its reputation seems to be in danger of swamping the music as crowds pack and overrun the establishments. If you are lucky, local farmers, fishermen and stone-masons will be providing the music. Two locals, Packy (died 1977) and Miko Russell, were among the best traditional musicians in Ireland.

Out to the Sea

The road continues out to Doolin quay and strand. Hammer-stones, axes and flakes were found here by the Limerick Field Club, in the sand-hills on the right bank of the Aille, pointing once more to

Fisherstreet Village and the River Aille.

The stump of Doonmacfelim Castle.

very early settlement, just as at Lahinch and Fanore. About two dozen stone-axes, including broken ones, were located in the one spot, possibly signalling a stone-axe factory. If you do find artifacts, please notify the National Museum or the Clare County Library, as every little piece helps build the archaeological jigsaw of our distant past.

Doolin Pier

The road ends at Doolin pier, which was formerly known as Ballaghaline fishing station. It is the nearest point to Inisheer, the smallest of the islands, some five miles (8Km) across the South Sound. The quay is a neglected spot with rusted ladders and an air of decay. However, as a daily commercial service is provided to the islands during the tourist season, the facilities will be improved. A start has been made with toilets and a carpark but, unfortunately, the Local Authority (Clare County Council) are not responsible for the pier. Acre-sized Crab Island is a little out from the stony beach, its coastguard hut a place for cormorants to dry their wings, not 'the ruined home of some long gone, holy man.'

Doolin Point

North from the pier, the walk out to Doolin Point, up and over those limestone blocks, is interesting. These cube and cuboid blocks teach their own geology lesson of how the terraced hills were formed. Away from high tide, but near enough to be sprayed, are drifts of sea campion and thrift (sea pink), interspersed with 'rust-colour cushiony clumps' of Irish saxifrage with its little white flowers. On any day this place repays those with time to relax.

Fisherstreet

Back at Fisherstreet we recross the Aille, turning left to meet its final tributary, the Cronagort Stream, which rises on the boglands below Doonagore quarries, 170 metres above sea-level. The banks of the river along here are good fossiliferous localities. A mineral survey of Clare in 1788-'89 must have set some hearts fluttering . . . "the beds and banks of the Doolin river and the other rivers that run . . . may probably yield cobalt. Irish diamonds are in great abundance in these rivers"!

Doonmacfelim Castle, another O'Brien stronghold, now a mere stump with a vaulted lower room, appears to the left; access is from a by-road in Fisherstreet. And on the side of the hill to the right, hidden in a clump of furze bushes, Fisherstreet Pothole – another Pollnagollum – gives no indication from the road of its vertical, 13 metre drop into the Doolin cave system. The wide opening is dangerous and in wet weather the floods below rise to within five metres of the surface. Although potholers have surveyed the main cave and all its tributaries, the system remains popular with all grades of enthusiasts. However, with air space frequently less than twelve inches (30cm) above the water, traffic jams below are unlikely. But don't be surprised if you see mud-covered, wet-suited figures on the road here, and at Aran View swallet, near the present church.

Knockastoolery

Continue up Knockastoolery (Cnoc an Stualaire, the hill of the gallan or high stone) to the earthwork on the highest point. This is partly artificial, with a fosse and outer ring, topped by a two metre standing stone and a fallen stone. The smaller stones, creating the impression of a circle, are probably modern.

Burial mound, ritual centre or habitation site? Its purpose remains a puzzle. Was it built to ward off evil spirits emerging from the pothole? Or has it anything to do with the Iron Age Barrows, three of which are a few hundred metres east from here, opposite Doolin National school? Whatever its function, Knockastoolery commands superb views. Sir Samuel Ferguson stated that he found a defaced ogham inscription on the standing stone; but everyone else agrees that the scars are natural, the result of weathering.

Judge Comyn and his Mines

The road right at the crossroads will bring you past Doolin school to a disused opencast phosphate mine, the entrance to which is beside a limekiln, a half mile (.8Km) from the crossroads. This was one of Judge Comyn's mines, which he successfully worked in the 1930/40's. Some 85,000 tons were mined before the Government, fearing a lack of imports due to the Second World War, compulsorily acquired the two main mines. Not getting adequate compensation, the judge sued the Government. The ensuing litigation, which occupied the courts for 41 days in 1949 and 1950, was a triumph all the way for the retired judge: he received well over £20,000, with interest.

His victory was short-lived however, as the State, seeing that he would have made such enormous profits, claimed most of the money in arrears of income tax. Unfortunately the State did not make anything of the mines, and work had ceased by 1946, as phosphates could then be imported more cheaply.

This is the shortest road back to Kilfenora, less than eight miles (12.9Km) due east. But our journey is not yet finished, and so we return to the crossroads.

Francis MacNamara and Doolin House

At the crossroads, the 'drainy lane' to the left, again crossing the Aille, brings you to the ruins of Doolin House. Under the bridge the river in dry weather,

The standing stone on Knockastoolery.

sinks once more through its limestone bed, reappearing on Doolin strand between high and low tide levels.

The lane winds around the walled garden of Doolin House, described as the summer residence of the MacNamaras of Ennistymon. However, it seems to have been their permanent home in the early 19th century. Francis, minor poet, thinker and talker, did use the house as a summer home in the second decade of this century. His daughter, Nicolette, in her book, 'Two Flamboyant Fathers' describes life at Doolin in fascinating detail. She tells of how her father's friends, both Irish and English, were encouraged to break all the old rules, of how nude bathing was encouraged on the strand. This made for many a good Sunday sermon. George B. Shaw was a frequent guest to Doolin, but as Nicolette says . . . 'it is difficult to think of Bernard Shaw naked without a snort of laughter: was he covered in freckles with a fuzz of red hair on his chest?'

Augustus John, the greatest portrait painter of his age, was introduced to the west of Ireland by Francis, and came to Doolin often, and of course became Nicolette's other Flamboyant Father. It was while at Doolin that John painted his first 'lonely figure of a woman keeping watch over an empty land', inspired by those women who acted as look-outs while the poitin stills were operating. Scenes at Doolin strand were also painted by John: the aquamarine sea with its foreground of grey rocks; and the upturned currachs, 'like rows of huge sleeping walruses.'

The house, says Nicolette, 'though quite large, was a modest building, with crusty mouldering walls, a slate roof and stone floors'. Like so many more, it became a victim of the troubled '20's. Destroyed by fire, the building stone quickly vanished, and the Land Commission redistributed the land. This lane continues seawards towards Caheradoon, which was the largest fort in the area, but is now demolished.

Church and Tombs at Roadford

We return to the main road to travel the short distance to Roadford, with its restaurants, pubs and post office, and of course, a bridge over the Aille. The track to the right, on the north bank of the river, leads to another of Judge Comyn's phosphate workings, and to the ruins of his factory,and then on to Toomullin ruined church.

Toomullin

The name Toomullin is a corruption of the Irish, Tuaim Linne, the burial mound by the pool. Together with the parishes of Killilagh and Oughtdarra, Toomullin formed the district of Tuath Glae, as it is called in the O'Brien rental of 1380. The ruins here, near a waterfall are late medieval with some decoration on the narrow trefoil east window. St. Brecan is the local saint, and his well is nearby.

The four Masters record an incident, which happened here in 1565, when Mahon O'Brien, who had settled on the Aran Islands, was murdered by some of his own people. As a treaty existed between him and the Galway merchants for the protection of that port, they sought to avenge his death by pushing the Prince of Thomond, Donal O'Brien, to assert his authority. Thus egged on, O'Brien captured the fugitives, brought them back to Magh Glae, and within view of the scene of their crime, "Hanged some and burned others, according to the measure of their guilt." Glae seems to be a family name.

Killilagh

Travel down the boithrin opposite the post office to visit the ruins of Killilagh church, prominently sited on a small hillock. The cut-stone monument outside the graveyard is an unused MacNamara vault, now – to our great shame – in general use as a cattle shelter and in a filthy state. If you can look inside, notice the stalactites or straws, forming on the ceiling.

The 16th-century ruins are thought to have been built here on an earlier foundation, possibly a ringfort-type enclosure. A small earthwork remains to the west giving some substance to this claim. Killilagh appears as a parish church in the 1302 papal taxation list as Cill Eidlach, and the Calendar of Papal Letters contains numerous entries in the early 15th century, pointing to unsettled spiritual administration. So much so that the papal claimant, John XXIII, reserved the living to himself. But as he was deposed at the Council of Constance in 1415, while the Roman pope, Gregory XII, was still holding out at Rimini, who is to blame for the uneasy conditions at Killilagh?

In 1903 the great storm knocked much of this exposed building, particularly a tall, lancet-type east window. The main wing, almost 20 metres long, may have been in use as a nave, with the south extension adapted as a chancel. A very neat arch, with chisel punching on the blocks, leads into this side-chapel, which has single ogee-headed lights in the side walls and a double light under a hood mould, in the south wall. The main door, in the south wall, had a holy water font in the left jamb. As is usual in such churches, the north wall remains blank.

Burials have all but ceased here, since the new graveyard, across the way at Knockfin, was opened. An interesting

Single ogee-head light at Killilagh

Double ogee-headed light, again with chisel punching on the blocks.

stone head with a biretta, probably used as a corbel, was removed from Killilagh in 1971, but, through good detective work by Etienne Rynne and others, it was returned to the neighbourhood. To prevent any further removal, a decision was made to display the head in the Burren Centre, at Kilfenora.

A Court Tomb

At the end of the lane, about a mile (1.6Km) from the post office, continue for 200 metres west, keeping distant Inisheer beach to your left. On the limestone crags you should find the remains of Teergonean court tomb: upright slabs forming an arc or court area, opening to the north, and more rocks forming a roofless chamber to the south. While agreeing that the site does leave much to the imagination, surely the thought that Burren people were buried here, with great ritual, some 5,000 years ago, makes the short trip down worthwhile.

These court tombs, or court cairns as they were called, are the earliest type of New Stone Age (Neolithic) communal burial, most likely predating 2500 B.C. They have a predominantly Northern distribution: three hundred and ten north of a line from Westport to Dundalk, with less than ten south of this. The tombs varied in shape and construction, signalling many migrations (colonies); they are generally trapezoidal, consisting of a burial chamber and an open court, hence the name.

The open court was designed to hold the mourners, or to act as the ritual area, prior to burial, while the chamber held the cremated or inhumed remains and the grave goods: in other words, both tomb and temple. As the main concentration of these tombs occurs near Killala, Sligo

The Court Tomb at Teergonean with Leagwee in the background.

and Donegal Bays, it is not unlikely that a small group of people from these areas ventured down the coast to this strange land near the cliffs of Moher.

From those excavated it is known that large scale hunting was carried on side by side with the rearing of cattle. The site here on the limestone, beside very good pastureland, (due to the glacial deposits over the limestone), and with the backdrop of cragland, must have appealed to the small colony. Also, and this is very important, the light, well drained soil was suitable for primitive agricultural methods.

So what we have here is the cemetery of a small community of pioneer peasant farmers, probably the first Burren settlers, as distinct from the mesolithic hunters on the coast. And how well they sited their tomb, between the cliffs, the sea and Leagwee, the prominent erratic 400 metres to the north.

Incidentally, the townland name, Teergonean, (Tir gan ean, country without birds), is a misnomer: while I was parked under the electricity wires in adjoining Doolin townland, a flock of starlings decided to respray my car.

The Glashy Ridge

This neck of limestone, from the court tomb to Ballinalackan, is known as the Glasha ridge. In the general district Westropp counted the remains of over 65 forts, many with souterrains, constructed 'of walls of small masonry and great slab covers . . . sometimes having side cells . . . in one case leading to a pit of water.' He further tells that a complex passage at Caherglasha, twenty metres in length, was wrecked in an attempt to evict a family of badgers. But, undoubtedly, there are many more souterrains awaiting rediscovery. Also on the ridge at Cahermacrusheen, there was a collapsed megalithic tomb, mentioned by Borlase, the Cornishman, in 'Dolmens of Ireland', which he wrote in 1897.

The standing stones at the Court Tomb which divided the Court Area from the Tomb.

Journey's end at Knockfin

Knockfin, *Cnoc Fionn,* the site of MacClancy's bardic school of the Middle Ages, is a half mile (.8Km) further on the main road, near where the Church of the Holy Rosary now stands. This recently modernised church – locally called Tooclae – was built in 1830, following the granting of Catholic Emancipation.

The family of MacClancy, Mac Fhlanncaidh (son of Flanncadh, flann meaning reddish), were the hereditary brehons to the O'Briens, and as such they were, up to the time of the collapse of the Gaelic order, very influential in Thomond (North Munster). Some law texts translated by them, and some extant decisions in contemporary legal documents have survived. Three members of the family are recorded in the AFM: Aodh Mac Baothghalaigh (in English this is Boetius, a common name in the family); Baothghalach Og; and Sean, Ollamh to the earl of Desmond (South Munster). The townland of Cahermaclancy, with its souterrained caher, pinpoints their seat, possibly prior to the building of the stronghold, residence or school here at Knockfin.

Their proud name is severely sullied by the hanging sheriff, Boetius, now a hate target from the late 16th century: this shyster, a man fluent in Latin, Irish and English, had made himself useful in the scheme for despoiling the Clare clans, using his position and talents to expedite legal robbery. Moving with the new order, he sat in the Parliament of 1585. The Lord Deputy decreed: 'that Boetius Clancy of Knockfyne, gent, in regard of his birth, learning and good bringing up shall have, hold, possess and enjoy . . . the said castle of Knockfynne with three quarters and a half of land . . .' (a quarter of land was 120 acres). We shall see the role he played, as high sheriff for County Clare in 1588, during the Armada crisis.

The family lost all in the Cromwellian Settlement; and at the Restoration, their lands were granted to Cornet John Gore. Subsequently, several members of the family were prominent in the defence of Limerick, during the sieges of 1690/91, and as Wild Geese in the Irish Regiments abroad.

Poll an Ionian

The road continues north by Aran View House, where, according to Frost, gold and silver relics of the Armada, were to be seen. A swallet hole, leading to the Doolin caves is to the right before you reach the house. And west, on your left, the Glasha ridge contains the cahers and souterrains, previously mentioned.

Just before you reach Ballinalackan, the cliff face, to the right, one and six tenth miles (2.6Km) from Knockfin, contains the entrance to Poll an Ionain, so christened as the ivy-covered cave, following its discovery in 1952, by the Craven Pothole Club. When one reads experienced pot-holers describe the 450 metres to the main chamber, as 'a horrible knee-wrecking crawl' or as a 'long and terrifyingly claustrophic crawl' what would the layman think of such an experience? Faced with such an obstacle, most of us will never see the largest stalactite in Europe – its height is variously given between 8 and 12 metres – which adorns the main chamber.

The Hangman's Hill

Back at Knockfin, our journey is almost ended. The road right takes you back to Kilfenora, via Lisdoonvarna. Our last stop is one mile (1.6Km) along this road, in Canavan's field to the left: Knockauna-croghera (Cnocan an Chrochaire, the hangman's hill), where the Spanish Armada survivors were hanged in 1588 by Boetius Clancy. Here the grave is now just a mound of earth and stones, covered with coarse grass. Boetius, as the High Sheriff of the county, had received orders from the Lord Deputy, in the spirit of the times, "To apprehend and execute all Spaniards found there of what quality so ever. Torture may be used to expedite this enquiry." This Boetius did with such gusto, that "so terrified were the people that water was refused at Kilrush and Liscannor to a vessel which weathered the gale, though an equal quantity of wine was offered for it."

Persistent tradition and legend insist that at least one ship was wrecked on Doolin strand at Ballaghaline, and, that the survivors were hanged here, within sight of Knockfin. One of the unfortunates was the scion of a noble Castilian house, and messengers arrived in a vain search for the remains, for reburial in Spain.

But these fields, which witnessed such sadness, now resound to the annual noises of an international folk festival. 1979 saw 20,000 young people over-run these shale fields, listening to and singing with the folk entertainers of today, during a long week-end in July.

And so ends this Burren journey. May I wish you slan abhaile, a safe journey home.

Appendices

SOME NOTABLES FROM NORTH WEST CLARE

Daniel Huony

Don Daniel Houny, Admiral of the Royal Navy of Spain, was born at Deely Bridge, near Kilshanny about 1683. In an admirable article in Dal gCais 5, the Rev. Litton sketches his 'long navigation'. From his humble beginnings north west of Ennistymon he joined the British navy in 1713, and then the Spanish navy in 1715 where he rose through the ranks, surviving the vicissitudes of battles and expeditions, to become admiral in 1760 at Ferrol. The climate there did not suit him, but it wasn't until 1766 that he managed a transfer to Cadiz, where he died in 1771, one of Clare's notable Wild Geese.

J. P. Holland

John Holland was born in Castle Street, Liscannor in 1841. His father, also John, had been appointed to the Coastguard Station in the village in 1831. The boy was educated in the local national school, and then spent a year in Ennistymon, until 1853 when the family moved to Limerick, where John continued his education at Sexton Street. Poor eyesight prevented him from taking any sea-faring job and he joined the Christian Brothers in 1858, teaching in various schools until he was dispensed from his vows in 1872.

Holland was fascinated by the sea and particularly with models of underwater vessels which he was convinced he could perfect. So in 1873, he moved to America where he continued teaching and designing his submarine, motivated by the hope that his vessels might one day sink British warships! At first the American navy rejected his submarine plans as 'the fantastic scheme of a civilian landsman'. But the Irish Republican Brotherhood financed Holland's one-man model, and continued with the necessary finance until the launching in 1881 of the *Fenian Ram,* a 31 foot long, 19 tons displacement submarine with a three-man crew. Holland's patience with the tests was not matched by the IRB who took the vessel from the designer, only to discover their inability to manoeuvre her. The *Fenian Ram* 'the intended scourge of the British Navy', never saw any warfare but survives intact as a museum piece in Patterson, New Jersey.

After many near hits, the Liscannor man finally perfected his design with the launching of the *Holland* in 1898; this was to provide the prototype for the first mass-produced submarines. John Holland, the father of the modern submarine, died in August 1914, a few days before the outbreak of World War One in which his perfected underwater weapons played a major role.

Aodh Bui Mac Cruitin

Hugh Mac Curtain (c. 1670 - 1755), poet, soldier, teacher and lexicographer was born in the Kilmacreehy area. Traditionally, the townlands of Carronduff and Laghvally were the patrimony of his family, distinguished for their scholarship and as hereditary ollamh (teacher) to the O'Briens. Hugh fought at the Siege of Limerick in 1691 and departed with Patrick Sarsfield for the Continent, where he served in the Irish Brigade under Lord Clare. He was also tutor to the Clare children in Paris, and tutor for a while to the Dauphin.

On his return to Ireland he coupled his teaching activities with that of poet, antiquarian and lexicographer. A defence of Ireland published against a government-inspired *Hibernia Anglicana* landed him in prison in 1717. While there he wrote a grammar on the Irish language. On his release he returned to Paris where he published his English-Irish Dictionary, a valuable record of the vernacular of the time.

Following the death of his cousin, Aindreas, in 1738, he returned to Clare to the post of hereditary ollamh to the O'Briens. He spent his remaining years in his native area, teaching and writing poetry. He is buried in Kilmacreehy churchyard.

Charles Lucas

Dr. Charles Lucas was born near Kilshanny in 1713 and became an apothecary in Dublin. At the age of 24 he published a pamphlet on abuses in the sale of drugs which led to reform in the law.

He became a fiery advocate of justice; his charges of corruption against officials in the city administration, coupled with his demands for parliamentary reform, forced him to flee to the continent in 1749.

He qualified as a surgeon and returned to Dublin in 1761, where he was elected MP for the city. He was a founder contributor to the *Freeman's Journal* and also published a number of political pamphlets.

It was he who first wrote the description of Kilcorney cave which is contained in *Gough's Camden.* He died in Dublin in 1771, at his house in Henry Street and his statue adorns City Hall.

Brian Merriman

Brian Merriman, the son of either a small farmer or of an itinerant stonemason, was born about 1749 in Ennistymon. By 1770 the family had moved to Feakle where Brian married and became a hedge-schoolmaster, subsidising this precarious living by renting twenty acres of land. At the turn of the century he moved to Limerick with his two daughters. There he was known as a teacher of Mathematics until his death in 1805. He was buried in Feakle Churchyard.

His long poem of 1260 lines, *The Midnight Court,* is described as the greatest humorous poem ever written in the Irish language. Certainly it was the most controversial piece of Irish literature: up to recently it drew official disfavour in translation, and probably drew social disgrace on its author in the original. In the poem the poet dreams that he is in the Fairy Court of Munster, where he is made to account, in no uncertain earthy manner to the women, for the failings of men, particularly in the marriage sphere.

The *Midnight Court* displays Merriman's mastery of four languages: English, Irish, Latin and Greek, with the oral tradition of the Gaeltacht very evident. Indeed, Frank O'Connor contended that 'Irish literature in the Irish language may be said to have died with him'.

Cumann Merriman, a society founded in 1967 to study the history and literature of Thomond, hold annual schools, in the summer at Lahinch, and in Ballyvaughan during the winter. These are both light hearted and serious, mixing scholarship with gaiety. Merriman would have approved.

Bibliography

GENERAL

Antiquities of the Irish Countryside Sean P. O'Riordain, Methuen 1953.

Shell Guide to Ireland Lord Killanin and Michael Duignan 2nd Edition, 1967.

A Guide to County Clare Shannonside Tourism and the Clare Tourist Council, 1978.

Statistical Survey of Clare Hely Dutton, Dublin 1808.

Ireland, Graveyard of the Spanish Armada T. P. Kilfeather, Anvil, 1967

Richard Heaton of Ballyskenagh, 1601-1666, Laurence Walsh, O. Cist. Parkmore Press, Roscrea 1978 (Biography of Ireland's first Botanist)

Survey of the Megalithic Tombs of Ireland Vol. 1, Co. Clare. R. De Valera and Sean O Nuallain, 1961.

Irish Families, Edward MacLysaght, 1957.

Archaeology of Ireland, Peter Harbison, The Bodley Head, 1976.

Diocese of Killaloe from the Reformation to the 18th Century, Canon Dwyer, Dublin 1878.

Dal gCais, 1977, '78, '79 the magazine of Clare, edited by Harry Hughes.

Their Friends at Court. James Comyn, London 1973. (Memoirs of James and Michael Comyn.)

The Fauna of Ireland, Fergus J. O'Rourke, Cork 1970.

O'Brien, J.D. Williams, Cork 1977

Two Flamboyant Fathers, Nicolette Devas, London, 1973.

Industrial Archaeology, Arthur Raistrick, London, 1973.

The Limestone Crosses of Aran and Clare, Liam de Paor in the Journal of the Galway Arch. and Historical Society, 1955 - 1956.

Irish Medieval Figure Sculpture, John Hunt, Dublin, 1974. 2 Vols.

The Armada in Ireland, Niall Fallon. London 1978.

Travellers in Co. Clare, 1459 - 1843, Edited by Sean P. O Cillin. Galway, 1977.

History and Topography of the County of Clare, James Frost, Dublin 1893.

History of Clare and Dalcassian Clans, Rev. P. White. Reprinted by Fercor Press, Cork.

Cameos of History, Clare, Rev. Bro. Galvin. The Clare Champion.

Clare Official Guide, Dermot F. Gleeson. Fogra failte.

Changing Times – Ireland since 1898, as seen by Edward Mac Lysaght, Colin Smythe, 1978.

Irish Health Resorts and Watering Places, Edgar Flinn. London 1888.

SPECIFIC BURREN BIBLIOGRAPHY

The noted scholar and pioneer fieldworker, Clareman, Thomas Johnson Westropp, between 1880 and 1920, wrote almost 300 papers on all aspects of heritage study. Most of these were published in the Journals of the Royal Society of Antiquaries and in the Proceedings of the Royal Academy. He published popular articles on the Burren antiquities in the first journals of the Limerick Field Club, 1897 - 1908 (now incorporated in the Thomond Archaeological Society and publishing the North Munster Antiquarian Journal).

T. D. Robinson's Burren map – surely the best local map ever produced in Ireland – and E. K. Tratman's large volume on the Burren Caves provide much information on to-day's landscape. These writings together with the six inch Ordnance maps remain the basis for any Burren study.

Ordnance Survey Letters of Co. Clare, John O'Donovan and others, 1838 on. Unpublished typescript on each of the civil parishes.

Burren Journey, George Cunningham, Shannonside Tourism 1978.

The Burren Region, Shannonside, 1976.

The Burren, A Guide, Edited by Gerald O'Connell. Shannonside.

The Burren, (typescript) Statistical and other data, 1977.

Introduction to Burrenology, Regional Technical College, Galway 1978.

Irish Walk Guides/2. The West, Tony Whilde, 1978.

Geographical, April 1977, The Burren Down to Galway Bay, by Daphne D. C. Pochin Mould.

North Munster Antiquarian Journal Volume XVIII, 1976, Stone Head from Killilagh, Co. Clare. Etienne Rynne.

Dal gCais 1977, From Poulsallagh to the Black Head, by Joe Heinrichs.

The Pope's Own Irish Parish (Liscannor) Clare 1920.

The Irish Countryman, Conrad Arensberg, American Museum Science Books, 1968.

Family and Community in Ireland, Conrad Arensberg and Solon Kimball. Harvard University Press. 1968

Biatas, Volume XXX No. 6, 7. Article on the Burren by Olive Donegan.

Inishkillane, Change and Decline in the West of Ireland, Hugh Brody. Chaucer Press, Suffolk 1973.

North-West Clare, Today – Tomorrow? William Nolan, 1977.

Lisdoonvarna Spa and some other Irish Watering places, E. D. Mapother 1878.

Handbook to Lisdoonvarna and its Vicinity, Canon P. Dwyer. Dublin 1876.

Holiday Haunts on the West Coast of Clare, H. B. Harris, Limerick 1891.

Place Names of County Clare, James Frost reprinted by Fercor Press, Cork 1973

The Festival of Lughnasa, Maire Mac Neill, O.U.P. 1962

Parochial Survey of Ireland (1814-1819), Mason W. Shaw.

The Bannerman 1979, Official publication of the Claremens Association in Cork.

Conntae an Chlair, Sean O h-Ogain, 1938

Ireland of the Welcomes

Listening in Co. Clare, by Arthur Dembling. Vol. 25 No. 5. *The Burren,* by Sean J. White. *O'Brien Houses of Clare and Limerick,* by the Knight of Glin. Vol. 27 No. 3. *On the Slate,* by Jim Robson. Vol. 26 No. 2.

Golf '79; Story of Lahinch Golf Club.

Foras Forbartha Reports

Preliminary Survey of Areas and Sites of historic and artistic interest in County Clare, January, 1973.

Supplement to above report, covering central Clare, September, 1973.

Preliminary report on Monuments of Archaeological interest in County Clare, Richard Haworth and Aidan Walsh. June 1973.

Flora & fauna

The Burren Flowers, Florence Donaldson, Folens, Dublin

Blathra na Boirne, (The Burren Flora), Filmstrip and notes, An Roinn Oideachais, Baile Atha Cliath, 1975.

Cara, the inflight magazine of Aer Lingus.

Ireland of the Welcomes, Bord Failte magazine, various issues.

Birds of Clare and Limerick, Irish Wildbird Conservancy, North Munster Branch.

A Tourist Flora of the West, R. L. Praeger. Dublin 1909.

Geology

The Caves of North-West Clare, E. K. Tratman. David and Charles 1969.

Geological Survey of Ireland, Explanation to accompany sheets 114, 122 and 123 (notes by F. J. Foot)

Geology and Scenery in Ireland, J. B. Whitton, Penguin. 1974.

Limestone in North-West Clare. The Beds above the Carboniferous by Frank Hodson in the Quarterly Journal of the Geological Society of London, Vol. CIX part 3 for 1953.

The Geomorphology of the British Isles – Ireland G. L. Herries Davies and Nicholas Stephens. Methuen 1978.

An Bhoireann: Rilif, Draenail, Lonnaiocht, (The Burren: Relief, Drainage, Settlement) Filmstrip and booklet. An Roinn Oideachais, Baile Atha Cliath, 1975.

Maps

The Burren, a map of the uplands of North-West Clare, Eire, by T. D. Robinson. This is the most comprehensive map of the Burren and is a must for any visitor.

1.8 inches to the mile.
½ inch map: Sheet 14, Galway Bay
1 inch maps: Sheets 114 and 123
6 inch maps: Sheets 1, 2, 3, 4, 5, 6, 7, 8, 9, 10, 14, 15, 16, 17

Other journeys

1. Burren Journey (published 1978) through the central Burren region, commencing at Kilfenora and heading north, via Caherballykinvarga, Noughaval and Corkscrew Hill to the outskirts of Ballyvaughan village. The journey joins the Corrofin road and returns south, via Aillwee Cave and the megalithic tombs to Leamaneh Castle.
2. Burren Journey West
3. The third Burren Journey will travel through the north-east of the region from Ballyvaughan, to Kinvara via Bell Harbour and New Quay, and then south to Carron.
4. The final Burren Journey will detail the south-eastern region around Kilnaboy, Corrofin, Cahercommaun and Glencolumkille.